FBI AGENT

By Geoffrey M. Horn

Reading Consultant: Susan Nations, M.Ed.,
author/literacy coach/consultant in literacy development

Gareth Stevens
Publishing

Please visit our web site at **www.garethstevens.com**.
For a free catalog describing Gareth Stevens Publishing's list of high-quality books,
call 1-800-542-2595 (USA) or 1-800-387-3178 (Canada).
Gareth Stevens Publishing's fax: 1-877-542-2596

Library of Congress Cataloging-in-Publication Data
Horn, Geoffrey M.
    FBI agent / by Geoffrey M. Horn.
       p. cm. — (Cool careers : helping careers)
    Includes bibliographical references and index.
    ISBN-10: 0-8368-9193-7   ISBN-13: 978-0-8368-9193-5 (lib. bdg.)
    ISBN-10: 0-8368-9326-3   ISBN-13: 978-0-8368-9326-7 (softcover)
    1. United States. Federal Bureau of Investigation—Vocational
guidance—Juvenile literature. I. Title.
HV8144.F43H67   2008
363.250973—dc22   2008010380

This edition first published in 2009 by
Gareth Stevens Publishing
A Weekly Reader® Company
1 Reader's Digest Rd.
Pleasantville, NY 10570-7000 USA

Copyright © 2009 by Gareth Stevens, Inc.

Senior Managing Editor: Lisa M. Herrington
Editor: Joann Jovinelly
Creative Director: Lisa Donovan
Designer: Paula Jo Smith
Photo Researcher: Kimberly Babbitt

Picture credits: Cover, title page: Shawn Thew/epa/Corbis; p. 5 Newscom; p. 6 Robyn
Beck/AFP/Getty Images; p. 7 Zuma/Newscom; pp. 8–9 © Greg Smith/Corbis; p. 10 ©
William Whitehurst/Corbis; p. 11 © Bettmann/Corbis; p. 12 © Greg Smith/Corbis; p. 15
Dorling Kindersley/Getty Images; p. 16 Laurie J. Bennett; p. 17 (top) © George Steinmetz/
Corbis; p. 17 (bottom) © Bettmann/Corbis; p. 18 © Anna Clopet/Corbis; p. 19 Steve Rouse/
AP Images; pp. 20, 22, 23 © Anna Clopet/Corbis; p. 24 Time Life Pictures/Getty Images; p.
25 Roberto Schmidt/AFP/Getty Images; p. 26 Jerry Hoefer/AP Images; p. 28 Mark Wilson/
Getty Images

Printed in the United States of America

1 2 3 4 5 6 7 8 9 10 09 08

CONTENTS

Words in the glossary appear in **bold** type the first time they are used in the text.

CHAPTER 1

ON THE CASE

A spy sells American defense secrets to Russia. A congressman takes bribes and stuffs the money in his home freezer. A baseball player cheats by using illegal drugs. A gunman wearing a ski mask robs a series of Chicago banks. **Terrorists** plot to blow up an airport in Los Angeles.

What do these real-life events have in common? These are the kinds of cases that **FBI** agents investigate.

What the FBI Does

FBI stands for Federal Bureau of Investigation. The FBI is a U.S. government agency. FBI agents solve crimes and enforce laws. They also protect Americans from terrorists and foreign spies.

The FBI is not a national police force. It does not investigate all crimes. Local police enforce local laws. These are laws that apply only in a particular city or town. State police enforce state laws. These are laws that apply only in a particular state.

The FBI works with local and state police. It also works with police groups in foreign countries. But its main job is to enforce federal laws. These are laws that apply to the entire country.

FBI agents seize evidence from the home of a man accused of spying for Russia.

The FBI may take over a local case when federal laws have been broken. For example, local or state police handle most murder cases. But if a **serial killer** is involved, the FBI may take the case. The FBI always deals with plots to harm the nation or its leaders.

Who Works for the FBI?

The FBI has more than 30,000 employees. More than 12,000 of them are special agents. Agents carry out investigations. They collect **evidence**. They question witnesses. They arrest people suspected of breaking the law.

Agents in riot gear deal with a hostage situation in Los Angeles, California.

Some FBI agents have more unusual tasks. For example, the FBI has **hostage** rescue teams. Their job is to save people who have been captured by terrorists or other criminals. The FBI even has scuba teams. These agents are expert divers. They recover evidence from rivers, lakes, and harbors. They also check piers and ships for underwater bombs.

About 18,000 other people work for the FBI. They help the agents do their jobs. Many of these workers have special skills. Some are good at science or computers. Others are excellent at foreign languages.

Is This the Right Career for You?

Do you like reading crime and mystery stories? Are you interested in police work? Do you enjoy solving puzzles? Are you good at asking questions? If so, a career as an FBI agent may be the right choice for you. As an FBI agent, you can help people by stopping crime. You can help protect the United States from its enemies. You can help enforce the law. You can work to make sure that lawbreakers get punished.

The Nose Knows

Not all FBI agents are human. In fact, some are specially trained working dogs! FBI dogs sniff out bombs, firearms, and drugs. A handler trains the dog to look for whatever the FBI needs to find.

CHAPTER 2
WHAT DO FBI AGENTS DO?

What is a typical day like for an FBI agent? "No day is ever the same," says an FBI agent named Dina. "You never know what challenge or opportunity you may be offered next. Have your passport ready because you could be on a plane flying to Paris to interview a person of interest. You could assist another office and conduct **surveillance** operations in their division. If that's not exciting enough, how about putting the cuffs on a **notorious** crime figure?"

What's in a Name?

The FBI's name has changed three times since it was founded in 1908.

1908 ◯ Founded as "special agent force"

1909 ◯ Bureau of Investigation

1932 ◯ United States Bureau of Investigation

1935 ◯ Federal Bureau of Investigation

FBI agents go through a target training exercise in Dallas, Texas.

Since President Theodore Roosevelt formed the special agent force in 1908, agents like Dina have been trained to be federal crime fighters. Roosevelt thought government could solve crimes by using experts. He wanted to fight crime by putting together a team of special agents who would be well trained and well disciplined. They would become experts in their field. Today, FBI agents investigate crimes that range from spying to computer fraud.

At a crime scene, many kinds of evidence are collected, photographed, and labeled.

Criminal Investigations

Today's agents must be highly trained. They also have to be science experts. All agents must be familiar with **ballistics** and **DNA** evidence. They must understand how to use equipment to gather evidence. For example, agents use ultraviolet light at crime scenes to detect invisible blood spots and fingerprints.

Bank robberies and murders are just a few of the crimes that agents investigate. In such cases, FBI agents must protect the evidence from outsiders. Agents take photographs of the scene. They interview witnesses and take notes. They gather evidence and

The Hoover Era

J. Edgar Hoover (1895 – 1972) was one of the most important people in FBI history. The Justice Department hired Hoover as a spy catcher in 1917. He remained with the agency and became its director in 1924.

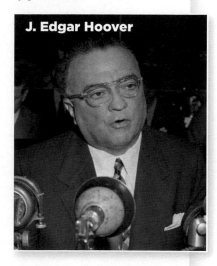

J. Edgar Hoover

Hoover improved how crimes were investigated. He started the FBI crime lab and the program of collecting fingerprints. Hoover also organized a formal training program for FBI agents that later became the FBI Academy.

Hoover was FBI director for forty-eight years. Late in his career, some people began to criticize him. They thought he held office for too long and had too much power. Since Hoover, the FBI director's term has been limited to ten years.

prepare it for further study at crime labs. Afterward, a report is made. Other evidence, such as fingerprints, will be run through the FBI's database to find matches. Working on a criminal investigation takes time and patience. Agents are trained to examine every detail.

Carrying heavy protective gear, an FBI SWAT team trains for high-risk missions.

SWAT Teams

Like state and local police departments, the FBI has SWAT (Special Weapons and Tactics) teams. These FBI agents are trained to handle high-risk situations. They may be called in to arrest heavily armed criminals. Sometimes they protect important people such as presidents. In rare cases, they may be used to control crowds during riots.

Hostage Rescue Teams

Some FBI agents are members of hostage rescue teams (HRTs). These agents are specially trained to rescue hostages. They may also be called in to fight possible terror plots.

Most members have backgrounds in **psychology**. Some are foreign language experts. They have knowledge of human behavior, helping them understand how criminals act. HRTs must be good at reasoning with criminals to prevent the loss of lives.

Cold Cases

Some cases take a very long time to solve. These unsolved cases are called "cold" because the evidence has provided few leads. Sometimes, unexpected details come out years after a crime was committed. In these instances, agents working in special units of the FBI will reopen the case.

CHAPTER 3

GETTING THE JOB DONE

Thousands of people work at FBI headquarters in Washington, D.C. But most FBI employees work elsewhere.

New agents are sent to one of the bureau's fifty-six **field offices**. These offices are located in major cities throughout the United States. New agents can ask to work in a particular city. But the FBI gets the final say. Agents are sent where they are most needed.

At Home and Overseas

The bureau has many smaller offices. These offices are called **resident agencies**. They are located in more than 400 small cities and towns. Each resident agency is attached to a field office.

In addition, the bureau has agents in more than sixty foreign countries. Some of these agents aid local police. Others work to protect American lives and property. In August 1998, terrorists in Africa bombed two U.S. **embassies**. The blasts in Kenya and Tanzania killed 263 people. More than 5,500 others were injured. The FBI sent agents to both countries to help find the people who planned the attack.

The FBI headquarters building in Washington, D.C., is named for J. Edgar Hoover.

High-Tech Gear

Fighting terrorism takes more than careful police work. FBI agents protect the public with the most advanced firearms and safety equipment. Some agents need full-body armor, night-vision goggles, and armored vehicles. They have the help of outside scientists who provide information, such as how to disarm a bomb.

On the Job: Agent Laurie J. Bennett

Laurie Bennett grew up on a dairy farm in Green Bay, Wisconsin, with her eight brothers and sisters. Before joining the FBI, she served in the U.S. Army. In Georgia, Bennett taught fitness to police officers and firefighters. She signed on with the FBI in 1990. In 1996, the FBI sent her to Saudi Arabia to investigate a bombing in which nineteen U.S. airmen were killed. She has also worked on other terrorism cases. In 2006, she was named to head the FBI field office in Buffalo, New York.

Crime Labs

In 1932, the FBI began using crime labs to collect and study crime data around the country. Today, the FBI has more than 40 million sets of fingerprints in its computers. In minutes, computers can match prints found at a crime scene with those of a known criminal.

FBI crime labs can also inspect traces of evidence, such as bits of cloth, fibers, and hairs, with high-powered microscopes. Other experts may examine the handwriting in a note or letter that was found at a crime scene. Even the smallest bits of evidence can help crack a case.

robotic arm

A robotic arm retrieves files from the FBI's huge collection of fingerprints.

Busted!

In the early 1930s, many criminals became famous. Some had colorful names like "Pretty Boy" Floyd and "Machine Gun" Kelly. Bonnie Parker and Clyde Barrow were robbers and killers. But Bonnie and Clyde were also media stars. So was John Dillinger. Each crime his gang committed made huge headlines.

WANTED

JOHN HERBERT DILLINGER

On June 23, 1934, HOMER S. CUMMINGS, Attorney General of the United States, under the authority vested in him by an Act of Congress approved June 6, 1934, offered a reward of

$10,000.00

for the capture of John Herbert Dillinger or a reward of

$5,000.00

for information leading to the arrest of John Herbert Dillinger.

June 23, 1934

To fight these famous crooks, Congress gave the FBI new powers. For the first time, agents got the right to carry guns. In June 1934, J. Edgar Hoover called Dillinger "Public Enemy Number One." A month later, federal agents killed Dillinger in Chicago.

CHAPTER 4
BECOMING AN AGENT

Becoming an FBI agent is difficult. When hiring new agents, the bureau sets very high standards. You must meet strict requirements before you can qualify for an FBI job. The bureau will do a complete background check on you. You must also complete a tough training program.

Students at the FBI Academy in Quantico, Virginia, learn the right technique for taking down a suspect.

A college student talks to an FBI recruiter at a University of Southern Mississippi job fair.

Meeting Standards

You must answer "yes" to all the following questions before the FBI will even consider hiring you as a special agent:

- Are you a U.S. citizen?
- Are you at least twenty-three years old?
- Do you have a four-year college degree?
- Do you have a driver's license?
- Can you go anywhere the FBI needs to send you?

These questions are only the beginning. You must have good eyesight and hearing. You must be able to pass a physical fitness test. You must also have some skill the FBI needs. For example, the FBI needs people with training in law and **accounting**. Several years of police work may be helpful. So is military experience.

The Next Step — A Background Check

FBI agents have a lot of responsibility. They can look at top-secret files. They carry guns. They are trained to use deadly force. The FBI needs to be sure its agents will not abuse their powers.

Before you can work as a special agent, the FBI will examine your character. Agents will ask your friends and teachers about you. You'll need to pass a lie detector test. You'll need to pass a drug test, too.

Good FBI agents must have high moral standards. To qualify for the FBI, you'll need a clean record. No serious crimes. No drugs. No bad debts.

All trainees at the FBI Academy must take a lie detector test.

Wanted: Accountants!

The FBI deals with many crimes involving money. Some crooks are very skilled at moving money around. FBI agents need to find the money — *and* catch the crooks who try to hide it. That is why the government needs agents who know accounting.

Here is a well-known case. Al "Scarface" Capone was a famous crime boss in the 1920s. His gang committed many violent crimes. Capone served prison time in the 1930s. Why? Because he failed to pay federal taxes on the money his gang made. The accountants battled Scarface — and the accountants won!

The FBI Academy

The next big step in becoming a special agent is the New Agents' Training Unit. "New Agent Trainees" are called NATs. Training takes place at the FBI Academy in Quantico, Virginia. For seventeen weeks, the NATs practice field exercises, study training manuals, and improve their physical fitness.

NATs spend much of their time in classrooms. They learn how to interview witnesses. They practice how to question suspects. Law is an important subject. So is learning the right way to enforce the law. NATs must pass nine separate exams on classroom subjects.

Work outside the classroom is also tough. NATs practice with pistols and other guns. They are tested on the accuracy of their shooting. NATs are trained to defend themselves. They learn how to control, search, and handcuff suspects. They practice boxing. They learn how to take away someone's weapon — and how to keep control of their own. NATs must pass a test in defensive tactics. NATs also must pass several physical fitness tests.

NATs who complete their training must then pledge to follow the FBI's core values. NATs pledge to obey the U.S. Constitution.

Target practice is an important part of FBI training at Quantico.

FBI trainees show off their street smarts when arresting a suspect at Hogan's Alley, a mock town built for training at the FBI Academy.

Hogan's Alley

The last test NATs must pass at Quantico is given at Hogan's Alley. Here, NATs put all their training and study into practice. Hogan's Alley looks like part of a city. A "crime" has been committed. Can the NATs solve it? They talk with witnesses. They confront suspects. They defend themselves against attackers. In Hogan's Alley, NATs show they can deal with the real world.

CHAPTER 5

MEETING NEW THREATS

FBI agents enforce more than 260 federal laws. The FBI became famous for cracking down on bank robbers and killers. But federal laws target many other types of crimes. For example, it is illegal to pollute the air, water, or soil. The FBI has squads of agents to catch people who poison the environment. Agents also crack down on some of today's biggest threats — fighting terrorism and computer crimes.

Most Wanted Terrorists

MURDER OF U.S. NATIONALS OUTSIDE THE UNITED STATES; CONSPIRACY TO MURDER U.S. NATIONALS OUTSIDE THE UNITED STATES; ATTACK ON A FEDERAL FACILITY RESULTING IN DEATH

USAMA BIN LADEN

Aliases: Usama Bin Muhammad Bin Ladin, Shaykh Usama Bin Ladin, the Prince, the Emir, Abu Abdallah, Mujahid Shaykh, Hu the Director

DESCRIPTION

Date of Birth Used:	1957	Hair:	Brown
Place of Birth:	Saudi Arabia	Eyes:	Brown
Height:	6'4" to 6'6"	Sex:	Male
Weight:	Approximately 160 pounds	Complexion:	Olive
Build:	Thin	Citizenship:	Saudi Arabian
Language:	Arabic (probably Pashtu)		
Scars and Marks:	None known		
Remarks:	Bin Laden is believed to be in Afghanistan. He is left-handed and walks with a cane.		

CAUTION

USAMA BIN LADEN IS WANTED IN CONNECTION WITH THE AUGUST 7, 1998, BOMBINGS OF THE UNITED STATES EMBASSIES IN DAR SALAAM, TANZANIA, AND NAIROBI, KENYA. THESE ATTACKS KILLED OVER 200 PEOPLE. IN ADDITION, BIN LADEN IS A SUSPECT IN O TERRORIST ATTACKS THROUGHOUT THE WORLD.

REWARD

The Rewards For Justice Program, United States Department of State, is offering a reward of up to $5 million information leading directly to the apprehension or conviction of Usama Bin Laden. An additional $2 million is offered through a program developed and funded by the Airline Pilots Association and the Air Transport Associa

SHOULD BE CONSIDERED ARMED AND DANGEROUS

IF YOU HAVE ANY INFORMATION CONCERNING THIS PERSON, PLEASE CONTACT YOUR LOCAL FBI OFFICE OR THE NEAREST AME EMBASS

October 2

The FBI launched a search for terrorist leader Osama (or Usama) bin Laden after terrorists destroyed the World Trade Center (right) in 2001.

Fighting Terrorism

Terrorists struck the United States on September 11, 2001. Nearly three thousand people were killed. Most of the deaths came at the World Trade Center in New York City. Other victims died in Virginia and Pennsylvania.

On the Job:
Agent J. Douglas Kouns

J. Douglas Kouns is an FBI agent who recently finished an assignment in Washington, D.C. He worked for the FBI division that protects the public from terrorists. Some terrorists have tried to use chemical weapons. Kouns knows a lot about these kinds of weapons because he studied chemistry in college. He recommends that students interested in careers in the FBI set themselves apart by learning a language. He encourages young people to set realistic goals. "We will all make mistakes," says Kouns. "What makes us successful is how we deal with them."

Law enforcement officials set up this computer lab in Dallas, Texas, to combat cyber crime.

The attacks shocked America — and the world. They also forced FBI leaders to do some hard thinking. Could the FBI have prevented the attacks? No one knew for sure. But one thing was certain. Like other U.S. agencies, the bureau knew it would need to do a better job. The top job of FBI agents is to protect the United States from terrorists.

Cyber Crime

Another growing focus of the FBI is solving computer crime, also called **cyber crime**. Cyber crime takes many forms. One type of cyber crime is called **phishing**. That's when crooks put together a fake web site that looks like a real one people know. People are encouraged to go to that site and type in their credit

Other Federal Crime Fighters

The FBI is not the only federal crime-fighting agency. Here are some others:

- *Drug Enforcement Administration (DEA)*: Enforces federal drug laws. Tries to stop illegal drugs from coming into the country.
- *Bureau of Alcohol, Tobacco, Firearms and Explosives (ATF)*: Enforces federal gun laws. Acts to stop illegal buying and selling of alcohol or tobacco products.
- *U.S. Secret Service*: Protects the president and other top U.S. officials. Enforces laws against **counterfeiting**.

The FBI Seal

The FBI seal explains the bureau's history and mission. Do you notice the circle of thirteen stars? They stand for the original thirteen states. The red stripes? They mean strength and courage. The white stripes? They suggest truth and light. The scales above the stripes stand for justice, as does the color blue.

The seal contains the FBI motto: *Fidelity, Bravery, Integrity*. Each of the three words starts with one of the letters in FBI. *Fidelity* means being faithful or loyal. *Integrity* means being honest.

card number. The criminals collect the credit card numbers. They then use the numbers themselves or sell them to other criminals. FBI agents are working hard to crack down on phishing.

Hackers also pose a serious problem. Today, all big companies rely on computer systems. Governments do, too. Some hackers act like cyber terrorists. They tap into these systems and steal valuable data. They also attack these systems and try to shut them down. Stopping cyber crime is one of the biggest jobs FBI agents face today.

FBI AGENT

OUTLOOK

- More than 30,000 people work for the FBI. More than 12,000 are special agents.
- The FBI needs more agents. But standards are high, and competition is very tough.

WHAT YOU'LL DO

- Your main job will be to enforce federal law and to protect the United States by investigating and fighting crime.
- As a new agent, you'll be sent to one of the FBI's fifty-six field offices, located in major U.S. cities.
- Every day is different. Some days, you'll be working at a desk. Other days you'll be out in the field looking for clues and catching crooks.

WHAT YOU'LL NEED

- A four-year college degree is required. You must be at least twenty-three years old and in good physical shape.
- The FBI will do a thorough background check on you. You must have a clean record. You will also need to pass a lie detector test and a drug test.

WHAT YOU'LL EARN

- Agents get a starting salary of between $61,100 and $69,900 a year. Experienced agents may earn up to $100,000 or more.

Source: FBI

GLOSSARY

accounting — a system for keeping and analyzing financial records

ballistics — the study of how bullets move and what happens to them as they are fired

counterfeiting — a crime in which something fake, such as fake money, is passed off as real

cyber crime — crime related to computers

DNA — a substance found in all living things that determines their traits

embassies — buildings where government employees carry out their official duties in foreign countries

evidence — the information gathered at a crime scene, such as fingerprints

FBI — stands for Federal Bureau of Investigation; an agency of the U.S. government that solves crimes that break federal laws

field offices — fifty-six main FBI offices located in U.S. cities

hackers — people who use computers to gain illegal access to other computer systems

hostage — a person taken and held by force

notorious — widely known for doing bad things

phishing — a type of Internet fraud

psychology — the study of the mind and human behavior

resident agencies — more than 400 FBI offices in U.S. cities and towns; also called "satellite" offices

serial killer — a criminal who, over time, murders several people in a similar way

surveillance — watching someone or something, often while trying not to be seen

terrorists — people who use violence to force other people or governments to meet certain demands

TO FIND OUT MORE

Books

Crime Scene Investigator. Cool Careers: Adventure Careers (series). Geoffrey M. Horn (Gareth Stevens, 2008)

FBI Agent. Virtual Apprentice (series). Gail Karlitz (Ferguson Publishing, 2008)

Law Enforcement. Discovering Careers for Your Future (series). (Ferguson Publishing, 2008)

Special Agent and Careers in the FBI. Homeland Security and Counterterrorism Careers (series). Ann Gaines (Enslow Publishers, 2006)

Working in Law Enforcement. My Future Career (series). William David Thomas (Gareth Stevens, 2005)

Web Sites

FBI Academy
www.fbi.gov/hq/td/academy/academy.htm
   Discover everything you need to know about the school where FBI agents are trained.

Federal Bureau of Investigation: Careers
www.fbijobs.gov
   Search for detailed information about FBI jobs, and learn why people joined the FBI.

Federal Bureau of Investigation: Kids' Page
www.fbi.gov/fbikids.htm
   Learn how the FBI does its work, including a day in the life of a special agent.

INDEX

About the Author

Geoffrey M. Horn has written more than three dozen books for young people and adults, along with hundreds of articles for encyclopedias and other works. He lives in southwestern Virginia, in the foothills of the Blue Ridge Mountains, with his wife, their collie, and six cats. He dedicates this book to all those who fight crime the right way, while honoring basic American freedoms.

home and away

home and away

A World War II Christmas Story

Dean Hughes

SHADOW
MOUNTAIN

Library of Congress Cataloging-in-Publication Data

Hughes, Dean, 1943– author.
  Home and away : a World War II Christmas story / Dean Hughes.
    pages cm
  Summary: Norma Hayes has always tried to make Christmas special for her family, but Christmas 1944 is especially difficult with her soldier son Glen away in Europe, and rationing and lack of money don't help. Teenage Dennis tries to buy his mother a special gift for Christmas as a symbol of times gone by and hope for the future, while Glen is reminded of home by the scent of lavender on a battlefield.
  ISBN 978-1-62972-093-7 (hardbound : alk. paper)
  1. World War, 1939–1945—Fiction. 2. Families—Fiction. 3. Ogden (Utah), setting. 4. Christmas stories. I. Title.
  PS3558.U36H58 2015
  813'.54—dc23   2015018652

Printed in the United States of America
Edwards Brothers Malloy, Ann Arbor, MI

10 9 8 7 6 5 4 3 2 1

To Chris Schoebinger

CHAPTER 1

Dennis watched his mother quietly walk to the kitchen table and set a pumpkin pie amid all the bowls and empty plates. Dennis pretended to be surprised—just to please her—but he had actually known for a couple of weeks that she had been saving ration coupons to buy sugar and eggs and lard. War or no war, Mom would never serve a Thanksgiving dinner without pumpkin pie.

Before Dennis could tell his mom how good the pie smelled, Linda was already whining. "Mom! I hate pumpkin pie. Why do you make it *every* year?"

Dad was quick to say, "That's enough of that, Linda! Don't talk to your mother that way."

Dennis understood his father's annoyance, but Dad didn't have to sound quite so angry. Lately, everything he said seemed to come out in that same tone of voice.

Still, Mom was smiling at Linda. "And what would you prefer?" she asked. "Apple, I'm guessing."

Linda glanced at Dad, and then she nodded resolutely.

"Well, let me look outside," Mom said. "There might be some apples on the ground under the tree. Maybe I can find enough to make another pie."

As Mom walked to the kitchen door and stepped out to the screened-in porch, Linda said, "I'll bet she already made an apple pie. She always says stuff like that."

"She's just teasing," Sharon said.

Sharon was six and Linda nine. The two girls looked much alike, but their appearance was almost their only similarity. When Dad barked at Linda, she shrugged it off, but little Sharon's lip would start to quiver, or tears would flow.

In just a few seconds, Mom was back from the porch with an apple pie. It had a beautiful slatted crust and sprinkles of sugar and cinnamon on top. The girls were pleased, of course. Dennis knew that Mom was trying to make the best of things, but it was a difficult day for her—for the whole family. It was 1944, and Glen, Dennis's big brother, was with the army's 101st Airborne Division, fighting in Europe. When the last letter had come from Glen—almost two weeks ago—he had been

at the battlefront in Holland. Newspapers were reporting heavy casualties among the Allied forces there. Linda and Sharon didn't entirely understand the danger, but Dennis did, and he feared every day that bad news might come.

The kitchen was warmer than it really needed to be, but it was cozy, and Dennis loved the smells of turkey and pie and fresh bread. He had eaten too much, of course, but he wasn't going to stop until he had a slice of each pie. Over on the kitchen cabinet, the radio was softly playing. A big band was performing "Santa Claus Is Coming to Town." The local station in Ogden, Utah, had begun to play Christmas music that day. When Linda started to sing the words to the song, Dad finally seemed to notice, and he groaned. "They start earlier every year," he said. "The stores must pay the radio station to play that stuff. That's all Christmas is now—a chance to boost sales."

It was what Dad said every year. But Mom loved Christmas, and she did all she could to make the holidays nice. Every fall she peeled tomatoes for a cannery in town, and all her "tomato money," as she called it, went toward presents and decorations. Dad did like to have a Christmas tree, and he always came up with a couple of dollars to buy one, but he didn't bother with the shopping and wrapping and all the rest.

Dennis had eaten his pie and was carrying his plates to the sink when he heard the news headlines come on. He stopped to listen. Almost everything was war news these days, but today the announcer read a brief Thanksgiving greeting from President Roosevelt, who had been reelected earlier that month for his fourth term. The news from the Philippines was that General MacArthur's troops were steadily advancing, taking back control of Leyte Island. But the next item was the one Dennis had been waiting to hear: "Fighting remains at a standstill in the Netherlands. The heavy losses that Americans sustained in the initial battle have slowed, but another thrust toward the Rhine could come at any time."

The thought of it—another attempt to attack across the border and into Germany itself—was frightening. The 101st and 82nd Airborne Divisions had parachuted into Holland in the middle of September. They had joined with other Allied troops and pushed toward Arnheim, across the Rhine, in a drive that had failed after a week of heavy fighting. Glen had written once after that; he had been all right at that point. But the boy had been through a lot in the last six months. In June he had been dropped into Normandy on D-Day. He had survived the battles that followed, and his unit had been

pulled off the line, given a short rest, and then had been sent to make a second drop, this one into Holland.

"They won't try to cross the Rhine right away, will they?" Dennis asked his dad.

Dennis wondered whether his father had even listened to his question. He was still sitting at the table, drinking a cup of coffee, seemingly lost in thought. He could be talkative at times, especially if he had drunk a few beers, but these days everything seemed to annoy him. "How am I supposed to know, Dennis?" he finally said. "The little news we get is mostly just lies."

"They wouldn't send the boys into Germany right before Christmas, would they, Hal?" Mom asked.

Dad slapped his hand on the table. "Norma, think about that. Do you think the generals give their soldiers time off for a nice little vacation during the holidays? That doesn't even make sense."

Dennis saw the hurt in Mom's eyes. She was used to Dad telling her she didn't know what she was talking about. He did that all the time. But Dennis knew what she was thinking. Christmas was important. Even generals ought to know that.

What bothered Dennis was that his dad understood so little about his mom. It never would have occurred to Dad to say, "I'm sorry. I shouldn't have raised my voice

like that." Dennis had never heard him apologize for anything, had never once heard him say, "I love you." Not even to Mom. Certainly not to Dennis.

"All I meant was—"

Dad stood up abruptly, pushing his chair back with a loud scrape. "I know what you mean. You don't want your son to get killed on Christmas Day. I'll send Eisenhower a telegram and let him know."

Linda and Sharon had wandered off to the living room, but now little Sharon was standing in the kitchen doorway. "What'sa matter?" she asked. "Is Glen okay?"

The room fell silent except for the sound of the radio: Singing star Dick Haymes was crooning, "O Little Town of Bethlehem."

"Honey, he's fine," Mom said. "It's nothing like that." But Sharon's eyes were full of the confusion that Dennis had seen so often these last few months. Glen was mostly a photograph to her. He sat on an end table in the living room. All Sharon knew was that he was her brother and that he was "in the war"—whatever that meant to her.

Mom went to Sharon, kneeled and hugged her, and told her that everything was all right, that she didn't need to worry.

Dennis could hear the song: "Where meek souls will receive him, still the dear Christ enters in."

Dennis thought Dad needed to say something to Sharon. But he didn't. He had walked to the back door, and now he grabbed his old coat off a peg and walked on outside. He was obviously heading out to the garage in back, where he spent a lot of his time. Mostly he puttered around with his old car, or he fiddled around on little woodworking projects. More than anything, Dennis believed, he preferred to be by himself. He also kept a bottle out there for times when he wanted something stronger than beer.

Mom stood and looked at Dennis. She whispered, "How do I manage to ruin every special occasion?"

Dennis walked to her and took hold of her shoulders. "Don't say that, Mom. He didn't have to talk to you like that."

"Well . . . I'm sure he's right. Generals have lots of things to consider that I don't know anything about."

Dennis thought of telling her that she was too quick to blame herself—that Dad was the one who was wrong—but he didn't want Sharon to hear him talk that way. "Well, anyway, it was a great dinner," he said. "You didn't ruin anything." Mom gave Dennis a little hug, and he caught a whiff of the lavender water she liked to wear. It was the smell of Mom, always had been.

Dennis carried the last of the dishes to the sink, and

then he said, "All right, women of the house, I want you to take it easy the rest of the afternoon. I'm going to do the dishes."

"You'll probably break half of 'em," Linda called from the living room. When Dennis turned to look at her, she stuck her tongue out. That was the sort of thing Linda always did. She didn't really do anything that was all that naughty—but she liked to think she did.

Linda and Sharon both had hair like Dad's—sort of blondish—but they had brown eyes, like Mom. Dennis was the only one with hair as dark as his mother's, but it was Sharon who had gotten Mom's flashy dimples. Dennis had dimples too—just not such deep ones. Still, people told him that he had his mother's smile.

Mom did let Dennis do the washing, but she stood at the sink with him, silently, and dried each dish. Dennis knew she was worried—probably about getting Dad upset and, even more, that he was out in the garage. If he started drinking whiskey, the day could get a lot worse.

The Hayes family lived in a little three-bedroom house in an old part of town, but the kitchen was bright, with white cupboards and red linoleum. Mom had brought a big oak dinner table with her from her parents' house in Wyoming, and that had ended up being

the center of almost everything in the family—that, and the radio.

After a time Mom asked Dennis, "Do you remember Thanksgiving the last year before Glen left?" He could tell where her thoughts had now gone.

"Yeah, sure. He was just getting ready to leave for the army."

"And now this will be his third Christmas away from us."

"We did that big jigsaw puzzle," Dennis said. "Even Dad worked on it a little. I think about that a lot: the four of us around the table and the girls playing on the floor. Glen would bust out laughing and say 'got one' every time he found a piece that fit."

But there was another part to that memory. Dad never did anything like that now. He had always joked around with Glen, like they were pals, but he didn't treat Dennis that way, and Dennis didn't know why.

Something else also struck him. He could still picture his mother across from him at the table that day, and she had been wearing the same dress she was wearing now. She had a gray church dress and this tired green one she was wearing now, and she had some faded house-dresses. Mom did everything for him and his little sisters and never spent a dime on herself. But Dennis had an

after-school job now; this Christmas he could get something nice for her. Maybe he could buy her a new dress. The problem was, a dress might cost more than he could come up with. He needed Dad to help pay for it.

So Dennis finished the dishes, and he waited until Mom was in the living room talking to the girls, and then he slipped out to the garage. As he walked to the sagging building with its peeling paint, he tried to think how he could ask his dad for money without getting him upset. When he stepped through the side door, he found his dad sitting on a stool, not really doing anything. He was smoking a cigarette, looking solemn, but Dennis saw no sign that he had been drinking. "Dad, could I talk to you about something?" Dennis said.

Dad nodded, but he looked anything but eager.

"I think everyone's on edge right now," Dennis began. "We're all so worried."

"No doubt."

"I think we have to be careful."

"Is that what you came out here to tell me? To watch my mouth?"

"No. But Christmas is going to be hard. Mom doesn't think about battle strategies. She just thinks about Glen."

"Well, what do you think's on *my* mind?"

That wasn't the reply Dennis had expected, and it

softened his feelings. He took a deep breath and went on. "Anyway, I was just thinking, we ought to make Christmas as nice as we can for Mom—you know, cheer her up a little. She hasn't had a new dress for a long time. She needs something nicer that she can wear to church. So I was thinking—"

"When's the last time I got a new suit?"

Dennis tried to think how to answer that. He could have said, "When was the last time you went to church?" but that would have made Dad mad. Or he could have said, "You live in your coveralls most of the time. Clothes don't mean a thing to you." But Dennis knew he had to tread lightly. "I'm just thinking, it would be nice if Mom had something to be happy about. Maybe you and I could go in together and buy her a church dress."

At least Dad didn't turn him down immediately. He sat for a time, took another puff on his cigarette. "That's prob'ly a good idea," he said—to Dennis's surprise. "What would it cost?"

"I don't know exactly."

"I can go five bucks, but that's pushing it. It's tough at the shop this time of year. Everyone's broke from spending too much on Christmas. They don't come in and get their cars fixed."

"Yeah, I know. But at J. C. Penney's I might be able

to get something pretty nice for ten dollars—if I put in five with your five."

"You can get a dress cheaper than that."

Dad never knew what things cost, but Dennis knew better than to say that. He only said, "Okay. That sounds good. Do you want to go look for something, or—"

"No, I wouldn't know what to buy. You know what your mother likes better than I do."

"All right. I'll look around. You know how hard Mom always works to make Christmas nice for us. For once, she ought to have something really nice herself."

Dad looked down at the cigarette between his fingers—just sat and stared at it for quite some time as a little column of smoke spiraled past his face. "You always find a way, don't you?" he finally said.

"Find a way to what?"

"You come in here all soft-spoken and full of love for your mother, and then you figure out a way to tell me what a louse I am."

"I didn't say—"

"I'm well aware that we don't live up on the hill where all your friends live, and we don't have a fancy house. I'm sure, in your mind, that's my fault. And now it's your mother's clothes. I don't buy her the fancy dresses that you think she oughta have."

"I didn't mean it that way."

"You haven't even told me yet that I better not have anything to drink this Christmas."

Dennis knew what his father was talking about. Back when Dennis had been twelve or thirteen, Dad had gotten drunk on Christmas Eve. He and Mom had gotten into a huge fight, and Dad had even walked out of the house and not come back until late that night. Since then, Dennis had heard his mom plead with Dad not to drink during the holidays, and Dad chafed each time she talked that way.

"I didn't have anything like that in mind at all," Dennis said.

"Oh, you had it in mind. You and your mother never stop talking, and I know exactly what you say about me: I don't go to church. I swear too much. I waste my money on beer and cigarettes. I don't have a decent job."

"Dad, we don't say anything like that."

But Dennis wasn't being entirely honest. Mom did worry out loud about Dad's drinking, and she did tell Dennis never to start smoking, that it was like burning dollar bills. And yet, she always excused Dad. "Well, he got started as a boy," she would say. "And it's just a really hard habit to break. I know he would like to quit."

"Dennis, I know how things are in this family," Dad

said. "You grabbed onto your mother's apron strings about as soon as you could walk, and she taught you from the beginning, your old man ain't worth nothin'."

"That's not true, Dad. Mom always tells me what a good mechanic you are—how you can fix a car when no one else can. And she—"

"Lay off, Dennis. You don't care if I'm a good mechanic. You're ashamed I'm not a doctor or a lawyer or something like that. But you know what? Glen always thought I was a pretty good guy."

"You are a good guy, Dad."

"I don't want to hear it, Dennis. I've known for a long time how you think about me."

Dennis wanted to deny whatever Dad was thinking, but he couldn't find the courage even to look him in the eye.

"When you were about the size of Sharon, I was getting ready to go to church, and you said, "Wash your hands, Daddy. You can't go to church with dirty hands.'"

"I was a little kid, Dad. I didn't understand how grease gets into your skin and—"

"But you understand now. And you still hate my hands." He held them up, palms toward Dennis, the cigarette still between his fingers. "Don't tell me any different."

The worst part was, Dennis knew it was true. He had always hated those hands.

"Go back in the house before I come over there and knock you through the wall."

Dennis gave up. He started to turn toward the door when Dad slid off the stool and said, "Wait a minute. Here's your five dollars—for you and your mother."

Dennis almost walked away. He wanted to buy the dress with his own money. But doing that would make things worse. So he took the five-dollar bill from his dad's grease-stained hands and said, "Thanks."

He did walk back to the house, but all he could think was that Dad was right about him, at least in some ways. And yet, Dad didn't really understand. Dennis had realized even as a little boy that his father didn't play with him, never touched him. And somehow, in his child's mind, it had seemed that Dad couldn't touch things because his hands were so dirty. He had wanted to sit on his daddy's lap, the way some kids did. He remembered climbing up once and sitting sideways across his knees, but Dad hadn't taken hold of him, hadn't hugged him. He had been stiff and uncomfortable, and Dennis had felt the same way. Dennis had never tried to get that close to his father again.

CHAPTER 2

It was still raining in Holland, as it had been off and on for two weeks. Early in the afternoon Corporal Glen Hayes's squad got pulled back from their foxholes a few hundred yards. A truck had brought in what was supposed to be a hot meal. "What's this?" Glen asked.

"Thanksgiving dinner," a cook said, his voice sounding muffled under the hood of a green poncho. He didn't look up. "Open your mess kit."

So Glen held out his mess kit, and a line of three cooks slapped canned turkey, canned green beans, and a blob of runny potatoes into the kit. A fourth man poured thin, gray gravy over everything.

Private Sid Dibbs, Glen's foxhole mate, was standing behind him in line. "Didn't you know that today is Thanksgiving?" he asked.

Glen had known the day was coming up, but he

hadn't thought of it so far today. "Isn't Thanksgiving always on Thursday?"

"Yeah."

"It's not Thursday, is it?"

"I don't know."

One of the cooks said, "Yeah, it's Thursday. We have to haul these meals to all the troops today. In this mud."

"Yeah, well, happy Thanksgiving to you, too," Dibbs said. "Why don't you take my spot on the line? I'll drive your truck for you."

"You don't know what a mess these roads are," the cook said, and then he cursed the rain and the mud, as though he didn't dare curse Dibbs.

"Try *living* in mud. We're dug in up there. We sleep in this muck."

"Who sleeps?" Glen asked, but the cooks were paying no attention. Glen walked a few paces away and stood by an open fire while he ate his turkey. It tasted like tin. Rain was splashing into his potatoes. What he could guess was that this food was some commander's idea of a way to bolster the morale of the soldiers: a real Thanksgiving meal, just like home. Never mind that the men were soaked through to the skin and there was no hope of getting dry. Never mind either that the stench of all that

17

mud, of overflowing latrines, of wet uniforms, fouled the taste of any meal.

The worst thing, though, was the reminder that to-day was Thanksgiving back in the States. Glen thought of his family sitting down in the kitchen at home, warm and dry, and Mom roasting a turkey, baking pumpkin pies. A realization had settled into Glen's mind lately: the odds were, no matter how much he tried to deny them, he would probably never see his family again. He would never again sit down to Thanksgiving dinner with them. His unit had taken a beating in Normandy and again in Holland, and he had come out unscathed. But how long could that continue? With so many men falling around him, it seemed obvious that his turn would come. He didn't dwell on the idea, didn't exactly despair, but it was the reality he lived with now.

The men of the squad took their time, standing as long as they could near the fire as it hissed and sputtered in the rain, but then Sergeant Caruthers, Glen's squad leader, told the men to move out. They hiked back to the front line. To Glen, the little break only served to make his situation seem more absurd. His unit had been part of a magnificent strategy when they had dropped into Holland. Americans, Brits, Canadians, even Poles would make a sudden surprise drive up a single road and across

the Rhine and then straight to Berlin. It had all sounded reasonable at the briefing, but that single road had turned into a traffic nightmare, with troops and heavy equipment bogged down—easy targets for enemy aircraft. In the end, some units had crossed the river, but most had not, and finally all Allied troops had had to withdraw.

That much, Glen understood. But now his battalion had dug foxholes and trenches, and they were bogged down in a standoff with the Germans. Neither side made major thrusts at the other, but sharpshooters sniped often enough to harass the other side, and occasionally artillery shells or mortars came crashing into camp, mostly just a reminder that the enemy was not far away. It all seemed pointless. The boredom and misery were bad enough, but a few men were being lost almost every day, and Glen could see no military purpose in anything they were doing. Then the rainstorms had come, and the mud was getting into everything and everyone, clinging to men's boots and clothes, turning all reality into an ugly shade of gray-brown. Glen had heard that some men had cracked up. One had made a mad run at the Germans, probably his way of committing suicide. A couple of others had been dragged off by medics, screaming, profaning, trying to kill the men who wanted to help them.

Glen wasn't ranting. He was turning inward. He

could feel himself shutting down. He had been trained to fight, to defend America, to win a war; he hadn't been trained to sit in mud all day, all night, and shiver in a wet uniform.

When Glen and Dibbs got back to the line, they used their shovels and even the cups from their mess kits to slosh some of the water out of their foxhole, and they built up a little ridge of dirt to keep more water from running in, but the rain kept coming, and there was nothing they could do about that. They didn't try to lie down. They simply sat, backs against the wall of the foxhole, shrouded by their ponchos. More than anything, Glen wanted to sleep. He loved to imagine a full night's rest in a bed. At home, he had slept in the same bed with his little brother, Dennis, and he had hated the way the kid rolled about and pulled at the covers. But now he shut his eyes and tried to imagine a warm bed, a mattress, sheets, dry blankets.

Glen held the hood of his poncho down over his eyes and then, with his arms across his knees, bent forward and rested his head on his arms. Something like sleep overtook him almost instantly. But it was the half sleep he had come to know so well—with images flashing around in his head, words, confusion, even nausea. He broke into wakefulness every few minutes, and then he

would slide back into the chaos of all those visions. At some point he realized he was talking out loud—shouting, actually.

"Corporal. Corporal," someone was saying. "Hayes!"

"Okay, okay."

All this had happened before. Dibbs had had to shake him sometimes.

"Are you okay?"

"Yeah. I'm sorry. I just . . ."

"I know."

Glen was awake now, fully, and he knew how this would go. He would be awake all night. "Can you sleep?" he finally asked Dibbs.

"I don't know. I always think I'm awake, but I drift off a little at times."

"How long can we stand this?"

"There's talk that they're pulling us out before long. We're supposed to get some R&R."

"There's always talk."

"I know."

With the poncho pulled over his eyes, Glen couldn't see Dibbs. He could hear Dibbs's muffled voice and the smack of the rain striking both ponchos. "A guy in Charlie Company shot himself in the foot," Dibbs said.

"He claimed he was cleaning his weapon, but everyone knows he just couldn't take it anymore."

Glen had heard about guys doing that. He had tried to imagine it. "I couldn't do that, Dibbsy. Could you?"

"No. I've seen too many guys shot up by the enemy. I'm not going to do something like that to myself. You ruin your foot and you're messed up for life."

"But I mean, could you aim at your own foot, pull the trigger, and then just deal with the pain?"

"Why. Are you thinking about doing it?"

"No. I'm just asking."

"Not a chance. I don't like pain. And when I get home, my girl's going to want me to dance with her." Dibbs laughed. "And you know me. I can cut a rug with the best of 'em."

"I don't think I believe that. You can't even keep your balance in this mud."

"So? Who can?"

Sid Dibbs was from Philadelphia. He had been telling stories about his high school exploits ever since he and Glen had trained at Fort Benning in Georgia. He claimed to be a ladies' man, and Glen sort of believed him. He wasn't exactly handsome, but he had a bold way of talking and moving around. Girls probably liked how confident he was. But he wasn't so brash now as he had

been at jump school. This mud, this waiting, was taking something out of him, too.

So they sat in the rain. Glen didn't sleep, and he was pretty sure Dibbs didn't either. But it must have been ten minutes before Dibbs said, "You were talking about Walsh again."

"When?"

"When you yelled. You said, 'Get down, Walsh! Get down!'"

"I know."

"You gotta let that go, Hayes. Just don't think about him."

"That's what I'm trying to do."

But Glen kept imagining Walsh's mother getting the news, and he thought about the picture Walsh had shown him of a girl back home who was supposed to be waiting for him. She had looked rather ordinary, but Walsh had shown that snapshot around like she was a beauty queen.

Of course, Glen didn't want to think about any of that. When Walsh came to his mind, he told himself the things he knew to say: the Nazis had to be defeated; Walsh had paid the ultimate price, the same as a lot of guys were going to do; it was just one of the realities of war. But at night, when he would fall into that state of almost-sleep, his brain would go back to everything. He

would see Walsh at the moment the bullet struck, see what had happened to him.

"Were you right next to him when he got hit?" Dibbs asked.

"Yeah."

"See, that's why your mind holds onto it. But you need to—"

"Walsh got careless. He stood up and stretched. And you know how tall he was."

"Don't start talking about it."

"I'm not. I'm just saying, he got careless. We didn't hear a thing all that day, and then, out of nowhere, one of those snipers pulled off a round and Walsh was gone. It was just a split second. That's all it took. He pulled his helmet off, and he stretched his back. I said, 'Get down, Walsh,' but he brushed his hair back, like he—"

"Glen, don't do this. Just don't think about it."

"I know. I've got to stop."

But in the night, he kept seeing it over and over: what the bullet had done to Walsh's head. He hadn't known that a head was just a thing that could blow apart. And his mind, for some reason, didn't want to forget it. The rain and cold kept Glen awake, but Walsh's head did, too.

He bent forward again, told himself he had to sleep.

Then he smelled something. It took him a few seconds to realize what it was. When the airborne troops had dropped into Holland, they had gathered up their equipment and marched to their assembly point. Along the way, they had come upon a vast field of plants covered in purple blossoms. The color was beautiful, but it had been the smell that had struck Glen. He had plucked a little sprig and sniffed it. Then he had shut his eyes and breathed deep, and what had filled his head was the presence of his mother. Mom had always worn lavender water as a perfume, and suddenly there he was, in the middle of a war, and his mom was right there with him.

Glen had tucked the sprig into the chest pocket of his paratrooper jacket, and when he had had the chance from time to time, he had pulled it out and sniffed it again. He had basked in the memories it created. In a strange way, it explained to him what he was doing. It brought back what he believed—how he had felt when he had gone off to war to protect his country.

The lavender had dried after a time, lost its aroma. Still, he had kept the sprig. Now, maybe it was the wet that had soaked through his jacket and brought the smell back to life. He bent his head even closer to his chest, under the poncho, and he took long, deep breaths. He thought of Thanksgiving again, and his family sitting at

the kitchen table. He told himself he had to get through this—no matter that the odds were against him. He had to be home for Mom's Thanksgiving dinner at least one more time in his life.

CHAPTER 3

On the day after Thanksgiving, Dennis was scheduled to work a full-day shift at Walgreen's in downtown Ogden. He usually worked there only after school or on Saturdays, but Christmas shopping had now begun. Mr. Littlefield, his manager at the store, had told Dennis to expect a busy day, but when Dennis arrived at nine in the morning, not much was happening yet. Dennis knew enough to grab a broom and start looking busy, but in a few minutes Mr. Littlefield walked over and said, "Dennis, since we've got a little time this morning, why don't we rearrange the men's personal items? I've been wanting to do that."

So Dennis worked with his boss. He passed along tooth powders and shaving soap while Mr. Littlefield decided where to place everything. The man was kneeling on the floor, checking out what he had done so far, when

Dennis decided this was a good time to make a request that he had been thinking about. "Mr. Littlefield, I just wanted to let you know, I'd like to work all the hours I can during the Christmas rush."

Mr. Littlefield raised his head. His wire-rimmed glasses were perched toward the end of his nose, and he looked over the top of them at Dennis. "I'm glad to hear that," he said. "It's hard to find enough help these days. I can use you about as much as you're willing to work. But don't let me get in the way of your homework. I know how your mother feels about that." Mr. Littlefield attended the same church that the Hayeses did, and Mom and Mr. Littlefield had served together on some committees. He certainly knew that Mom had big things in mind for Dennis's future.

"I can manage plenty of hours between now and Christmas," Dennis said. "I need to make some extra money if I can."

"You must have a girlfriend." Mr. Littlefield grinned with a straight row of tiny teeth.

"Actually, I don't." Dennis thought about telling Mr. Littlefield about buying a dress for Mom, but that embarrassed him too much, so he just said, "I have some Christmas shopping I want to do."

"Well, that's good. What if I scheduled you every day

after school and all day on Saturdays? Would that be too much?"

"That's perfect. I could also work during the sales after Christmas, while I'm out of school."

"Oh, good. That's what I was hoping."

Dennis really was pleased. Besides getting something for Mom, he needed to buy Christmas gifts for his sisters and for Dad. When Glen had been sixteen, the same age Dennis was now, he had bought presents for the whole family. Dennis told himself he needed to be more like that.

As long as Dennis could remember, he had wanted to be like Glen. His big brother was good at everything, and he was well-liked, but a lot of guys Glen's age were kind of hard on their little brothers. Glen hadn't been like that. He would go outside with Dennis and throw a football or baseball around, and sometimes he'd taken Dennis to movies or skating at the roller rink—things like that. Since Glen had left for the army, the house had always seemed empty, and Dennis wondered every day whether he was still all right. He prayed for Glen every morning when he first got up, and sometimes he would say silent prayers when he was sitting in a class at school—or especially after school as he walked down the hill to his home or to work.

"What do you hear from the ol' paratrooper these days?" Mr. Littlefield asked. He knew Glen's name, of course, but he was especially impressed that Glen had qualified for an airborne division.

"We haven't heard anything for a while. We think he's still in Holland, but we're not even sure of that."

"Well, I can understand why your mom's worried. It's the same in so many families now. My sister's son is fighting the Japs in the Pacific. Her other son was in the marines, but he got lucky. He got himself a million-dollar wound. He'll be home before long."

"What's a million-dollar wound?"

"That's what a soldier calls it when he gets hit bad enough to take him out of the war but not so bad that it cripples him. Soldiers start to hope for a wound like that after they've been out there on the front lines for a while."

Dennis didn't like the sound of that. Mr. Littlefield obviously wasn't very patriotic. What he heard most people say was that American boys were ready and willing to give their lives for their country. They understood that freedom doesn't come for free.

"War is worse than anything you can imagine, Dennis. I was in the Great War. But I was fortunate. I never got sent to the front."

Mr. Littlefield looked more like a librarian than a warrior. He had a bald head and spindly arms, like the legs of a spider. It didn't surprise Dennis that a guy like that had been glad to stay out of the shooting. Dennis couldn't resist saying, "Some guys say they *want* to be at the front. They want to do their part, no matter how hard it is."

"People *say* a lot of things. But I'll tell you what. Everyone's scared when bullets start flying—or artillery shells are dropping in. Then all they hope is that they'll survive and be able to make it home."

Dennis understood that soldiers wanted to make it home, but brave men still did what they had to do. His buddies at school said that American boys wanted to march into Berlin and strangle Hitler with their bare hands. It seemed wrong to talk about soldiers wanting to get shot so they could get out of the war.

"I was assigned to an aid station," Mr. Littlefield said. "I watched the ambulances bring in boys who were all shot up and . . ." Suddenly he seemed to realize that he was saying the wrong thing to Dennis right now. He pushed a box of toothbrushes into place, and then he looked over his glasses again. "I'm just saying, I saw all the action I wanted to see at that aid station. That's how most of us felt—at least, all the ones who were honest."

Dennis didn't want to hear any more. He picked up a box of shaving brushes and held it out to Mr. Littlefield. The store was getting a little busier. He hoped his manager would notice and set this little project aside before long. He wanted to put up a Christmas tree, wanted to smell it, wanted that faint medicinal odor to disappear. But mostly, he didn't want to hear about wounds.

"Here's the thing I'd tell you, Dennis. Don't sign up any sooner than you have to. Wait until you get drafted, and pray every day that the war is over before that happens. War changes people, and usually not for the good. Stay out of it if you possibly can."

"I don't look at it that way, Mr. Littlefield," Dennis said, his words coming out louder than he had intended. "I'm ready to carry my share of the load, the same as any other good American."

What Dennis knew was that when he turned seventeen in the fall, he was planning to enlist right on his birthday, and he didn't want to show up at the recruiting office with doubts in his mind. Americans couldn't let men like Hitler and Tojo take over the world. Dennis not only wanted to join the army, he wanted to be a paratrooper, the same as Glen.

"Young men your age want to be heroes, not kids,"

Mr. Littlefield said. "But I'm telling you, you'll be better off if you never find out what happens on a battlefield."

That was easy to say, but Dennis knew that if he didn't go, people would ask him all his life what he had done in the war and he would have to say, "I went to high school and worked in a drugstore, and I stalled as long as I could and never ended up going." Instead, he was going to say, "Me and my brother, we both served in the paratroopers. We did our part." Still, he would be humble about it and not brag. That was how Glen had been when he got leave after jump school. He had come home with his pants tucked into his jump boots and bloused out, the way all the airborne guys wore them, and everyone had stared at him like he was already a war hero. But he hadn't been a show-off, hadn't made a big deal of himself.

Mr. Littlefield finally looked around and realized what was happening in the store. He stuck some boxes in wherever he could and told Dennis to work on getting the rest of the area organized whenever he got time. But there was little opportunity for that. Dennis waited on people, tidied up shelves, and directed customers to find things. He also did some calculating. He tried to figure out how many hours he would work during the holidays, and how big his check would be. He thought he could

get something nice for Mom and still have money left. At the end of the summer, he had put away some savings for his college fund, but he had ended up buying his own school clothes, and there wasn't much left in his account. Mom kept reminding him to put a little away whenever he could.

Santa was coming to the drugstore that day, and already mothers had started to show up with their kids. Mr. Littlefield had also hired members of the high school choir to sing carols: "Away in a Manger," "Frosty the Snowman"—everything. They sounded good, and Dennis knew most of the singers. He liked the music and the bustle, and he liked the sound of people talking and laughing.

Dennis eventually returned to the reorganizing project Mr. Littlefield had given him. He was bent over, looking to see what else he could do, when he heard a feminine voice. "Dennis, is that really you?"

Dennis looked up to see Judy Kay McCune, a girl he knew at school. She had sounded a little breathy, maybe nervous, but she was smiling, looking sort of sly. He had noticed at school that she had "happened to bump into him" a lot lately. She would show up at a nearby table in the lunchroom and then say, "Oh, hi," like she hadn't expected to see him. Besides, a friend of hers, Patty Doxey,

had asked him one day whether he liked Judy Kay. "Let's see," Dennis had said. "Is she about six-foot-six, with knock knees and a missing tooth in front?"

"Stop it!" Patty had told Dennis, and she had pretended to sock him in the jaw. "You know very well who Judy Kay is. You've known her since kindergarten."

Actually, it had only been since fourth grade. But that was part of the problem. Judy Kay had been an annoying little girl who had always said she hated boys and hated Dennis "most of all." He had never thought of "liking" her. And yet, she had changed a great deal in the last year. What had never occurred to him back in elementary school was that she would be pretty someday.

Dennis had even thought about responding to Judy Kay's attentions, but there were just too many reasons not to do that. For one thing, her family was rich, and she lived on "the bench," as everyone in Ogden called the foothills of the Wasatch Mountains. Dennis wasn't sure that Judy Kay knew where he lived, or what she would think of his house if she ever saw it. His biggest problem, though, was that he had no way to take her out on a date. He didn't have transportation, and his dad wasn't about to let him use the family car.

"So, how long have you been working here, Dennis?"

It was a simple enough question, but she was still

smiling, and she was blushing just a little—for no reason he knew of. He found himself struggling to concentrate on her question. "I started in the summer," he said. "I usually work only two or three days a week, but right now I'm working more."

"Oh. Well, it seems like a good job. You like to talk to people, and you're *always* friendly." She still sounded nervous.

"Yeah, it works out okay," he said. He couldn't stop smiling back at her, and he felt stupid. He tried to think of something else to say. "Actually, I asked for some extra hours during the holidays. You know, so I'd have some money for Christmas shopping."

"Oh, that'll be nice."

"Well, thanks for saying hello," Dennis said. He bent and looked at the shelf again. Mr. Littlefield always told employees not to waste time with friends who came into the store.

"So, who are you taking to the Christmas dance?"

"Me? No one. I'm not going." He stood straight again and looked to see her reaction.

Judy Kay had a light complexion, with creamy skin and round blue eyes. But right now her face was glowing pink, as though she knew that she had just crossed

the line and become a bit too obvious. "Really?" she said. "Why don't you want to go?"

"For one thing, I'm about the world's worst dancer."

She gave him a little slap on the shoulder. "Oh, that's not true," she said. Dennis knew nothing about flirting, but he was pretty sure that was what was happening right now. What surprised him was how much he liked it, and he was equally surprised at how much he liked looking at Judy Kay. Something had happened to the girl.

"Now, tell me really," Judy Kay said, "why aren't you going?"

"I don't know. I've actually never gone to a dance—except for those teen dances at my church. I've never asked a girl out in my whole life."

"You just need a good dance teacher." She held her arms up in dance position.

He knew what she was saying, but he couldn't do this. "I don't have a car, Judy Kay," he said.

"We could . . ." And then she hid her face with her hands. "I can't believe I said that. I meant, *you* could double-date."

"Well, sure, but . . ." He was trying to remember. There had to be other reasons not to let this go any further, but she had almost asked him on a date, and he found himself really liking that. He flashed his own smile,

and he said, "So what are you saying, Judy Kay? Are you asking me to go to the dance with you?"

"Dennis! I wouldn't do that. It's a boys' choice dance. The only girls' choice dance is on Valentine's Day. If you're trying to get me to ask you to that, I can only say I'd have to think about it." And then she actually winked at him. "For about two seconds, anyway."

"I'm not trying to—"

"Dennis, I'm sorry I've given you the wrong idea about me. I think I better go now." But her eyes never left his, and she didn't turn to leave.

"So, okay," Dennis said, "take two seconds right now and decide whether you want to go to the Christmas dance with me."

"Are you really asking me?"

"Well . . . yeah. If we can find someone to double-date with."

"Okay. One second. Two seconds. Yes!"

Now they were both grinning, and Dennis was thinking she was just about the cutest girl he had ever seen. "Well, okay, I guess it's a date."

"And you said you've never asked a girl out. It turns out, you're very good at it. I'll bet you'll be a good dancer, too."

"Really, I'm not."

"Well, I hope you don't think I'm too forward. I really am embarrassed. But Dennis, I've been hoping for a long time that you would ask me out." And now her smile was full and warm.

Dennis nodded; he couldn't think what to say.

"I actually know someone we can double with," she added.

"Oh, good."

And then she was gone. Dennis was left feeling as though she had pulled a plug on him. His strength was draining away.

CHAPTER 4

Dennis worked until five that afternoon. He was relieved when he finally got away from the store. The place had gotten much too busy. But as he walked up the 27th Street hill on that cool evening, he was no longer excited about his date with Judy Kay. The longer he had had time to think, the more he had recognized the problem he had created for himself. He really had nothing he could wear to a dance like that. He had seen the posters at school, and he knew it was a "best dress" event. That meant dressing up in a suit, and Dennis had grown so much taller in the last year that his old suit didn't fit.

A suit, if he bought one, would cost a lot, and he would also have to buy tickets to the dance as well as a corsage. Plus, most guys took their dates out for dinner after the dance. He couldn't just take a girl like Judy Kay to a hamburger place.

Dennis made up his mind. He was going to call Judy Kay and tell her that he had forgotten about a "previous engagement," or something of that sort, and couldn't take her to the dance after all. He wouldn't mention this whole thing to his mother; he would just wait until he could get to the phone with no one around.

When Dennis got home, he stepped into the kitchen. Mom was standing at the big, black coal stove, stirring something in a pan. "Hi, Mom," he said.

His mother turned from the stove and smiled. Then, instantly, her face changed. "What's wrong?" she asked.

"Nothing."

"Something is."

"It was just a busy day. I'm tired."

"I know that look on your face, Dennis. What's happened?"

He let the breath flow out of him; he knew he couldn't lie to her. "I did something stupid, Mom. I've got to figure out some way to fix it." She watched him, waiting. "Judy Kay McCune came into the store today. She hinted around about wanting to go to the Christmas dance, and the next thing I knew, I'd asked her to go, but—"

"Oh, Dennis, that's wonderful. I know who she is. She's about the cutest little thing who ever lived."

Dennis couldn't resist smiling. "Yeah, well, she's cute all right. But—"

"So what's the problem?" And then it hit her. "Oh. Your suit doesn't fit."

Mom was wearing a blue housedress, faded to a color close to gray. All he could think was how much he needed to buy a dress for her. She folded her arms across her middle, sort of gripped herself, and he knew she was trying to find an answer to his problem.

"Do you have any money saved up?" she asked.

"Just my so-called college fund."

"How much?"

"I'd have to check. But it's somewhere around fifteen dollars."

She was thinking again. "I have my tomato money," she finally said.

"But that's for Christmas."

"What if Santa gave you a suit for Christmas—and gave it to you early?"

"That wouldn't be fair. You don't spend that much on the girls. Besides, Dad would blow his top."

"You're working extra hours during Christmas. You'll be getting a bigger check than usual."

"Yeah." But he couldn't explain to her what he had in mind for that.

"Well, you come up with what you can, and I'll pay the rest. That's all we'll tell your dad."

Dennis never thought much about whether it was wrong to keep things from Dad. It was Mom's way of managing as best she could without confronting him. But nothing would upset Dad so much as the two of them conspiring to pull the wool over his eyes.

"How much do you think a suit will cost?" Mom asked. "A nice one."

"At Penney's, we might be able to get one for twenty-five, or somewhere around there."

"I want this suit to be really nice. I want you to look as good as any of the boys." She smiled, her dimples appearing. "Which means you'll look better—since you're the best-looking boy in the whole high school."

"Oh, sure."

"Judy Kay thinks so. That's why she asked you."

"She didn't ask me. I asked her."

"Keep believing that, sweet pea, but let's face it, you were putty in her hands."

That much he understood.

She glanced at the clock—one of those cat-shaped kitchen clocks with a swinging tail. "The stores are staying open late tonight. As soon as dinner's finished, you and I are walking back to town."

"I can go look around first, and then maybe—"

"No. You'll pick out something cheap, just to save the money."

"Mom, no offense, but I don't want my mother with me when I'm shopping in a men's department. That's what little boys do." Dennis saw the little hurt in his mom's eyes, and he quickly added, "It's not that I don't appreciate it. I just—"

"No, I understand. I have to get used to the idea that you're grown up. But I want you to buy something well made—and something that fits you right."

"I'll tell you what. I'll call Gordon. He's one of the best-dressed guys I know. If he goes with me, I can promise you, he won't let me choose anything but the best."

"But you can't spend *too much,* either."

"I know. I'll use my head."

"All right. I know you will."

So Dennis called Gordon Herrmann. He was one of those guys Dad didn't like: a rich friend who lived "up on the hill." His father owned a jewelry store in town. Gordon even had his own car—a '38 Chevy coupe, painted red.

"Hey, great," Gordon said on the phone. "I'm your man, if we can go early. I've got a date later on. But tell me this. Who are you taking to the dance?"

"Judy Kay McCune."

"Dennis! You're kidding me. How did you get up the nerve to ask her?"

"I don't know. I just . . . did."

"Hey, man. You're swinging for the fences your first time up to bat. I'm proud of you. But you've got to look your best, man. It's lucky you called me."

"The thing is, I can't spend a lot of money. Do you think we can find something at J. C. Penney's?"

"Uh, well . . . I doubt it. But we can look there if you really want to."

That worried Dennis, but he agreed to have Gordon pick him up in an hour.

Dennis was still finishing his supper when he heard Gordon out in front honking his horn. He shoveled in the last of his mashed potatoes and green beans and washed them down with a gulp of water. "I'm going to do some Christmas shopping tonight," he told his dad, and then he got up from the table.

Dad may have given a little nod. He obviously wasn't paying much attention.

Downtown Ogden was busy. Gordon had to make a loop around a block before he found a parking spot, which happened to be close to Walgreen's. Santa was still

there, and Dennis could see through the windows that the place was packed with people.

Penney's was on the next corner, so the boys started in that direction, but as they passed L. R. Samuels, a ladies' apparel store, Dennis suddenly stopped. "Wow. Look at that dress," he said. A dress in the window, on a mannequin, looked almost out of place. It wasn't dark like the other winter dresses; it was sort of purple, sort of blue, and it seemed to glisten in the floodlights that were directed on it from above.

"Yeah, that's nice," Gordon said.

"I want to get a dress for my mom for Christmas," Dennis said. "Something she can wear to church."

"That's a beauty, all right, but you better have a wallet full of cash if you're going to shop at Samuels."

"I know. I can't afford it. But I'd sure like to find something like that."

"And you want to buy a suit at Penney's?"

Dennis was reminded one more time that he had to hold onto as much money as he could if he wanted to have enough left to shop for his mom.

Penney's turned out to be busy too. Glen and Gordon looked through the suits they thought might fit, and a clerk kept nagging Dennis to try one on, but Gordon would say, "That thing is cut like a mailman's

uniform. The cloth is an inch thick." Or, "Dennis, that flimsy thing would fall apart in a month. No wonder it's only twenty-two dollars." He finally said, "Let's get out of here. I knew from the beginning we'd end up at Fred M. Nye's."

"Gordon, I can't afford that."

"Let's just go see. You can't walk Judy Kay into the dance looking like some down-on-his-luck traveling salesman."

So they crossed the street and entered into another world. The Fred M. Nye store was not nearly so busy, but the elegance of the place was almost frightening. Dennis was wearing dress pants and a school shirt, but his shoes were worn and cracked. He wished he had taken the time at least to polish them. A man who seemed like a butler from an English movie recognized Gordon immediately and asked about his father. He took Dennis's measurements and then politely held coats out for Dennis to slip into. He seemed to understand that he couldn't show him the most expensive choices, but he didn't make him feel out of place, either.

When Dennis tried on a blue serge, Gordon said, "Hey, that's the number. You look like Cary Grant. Wear that, and Judy Kay won't trade a dance the whole night."

"How much is it?" Dennis asked. He tried to sound as though the price didn't matter very much.

"Thirty-eight dollars, sir. But we're offering your choice of any tie to go with it."

Thirty-eight dollars. Dennis didn't think he could swing that. Mom had given him forty dollars, but he had promised to pay at least twenty of it back when he withdrew his savings and got his next paycheck.

"That's a *bargain,* Dennis," Gordon said. "You can't do any better than that—not for a quality suit."

"That's certainly true," the salesman said.

Dennis didn't know what the other suits cost. He glanced around to see if there was something he liked almost as well, but he was too embarrassed to ask the prices.

"Why don't you try on the trousers with it?" the man said.

Dennis was glad for the time to think, but he was still feeling self-conscious about saying he couldn't afford it. When he stepped from the dressing room, he turned toward the mirror and took another look. He had never seemed so grown-up, so classy, in his life. He wanted that suit. Suddenly he made the decision. He had enough money in his pocket; he would buy it and figure out the rest of his finances later.

"Okay, I'll take it," Dennis said.

"Great choice," Gordon said. "I told you I was your man."

The salesman crouched and pinned the pant legs at the right length, then said, "Have you thought about shoes?"

Dennis took a breath.

"I hate to say this, Dennis," Gordon said, "but there's no way you can wear those shoes to the dance—not with that suit."

Dennis knew he was already in over his head, but he also knew Gordon was right. "I didn't bring enough money with me," he said. "Maybe I could come back later and—"

"If you like," the salesman said, "you can choose your shoes now, and we can lay them away for you until you can return and pay for them."

Dennis knew he shouldn't do it, but he felt like a man of the world when he said, "Well, sure. We could handle it that way."

So Dennis picked out a pair of shoes—nice wing-tips—that cost eight dollars. He tried to think how he could pay for everything, but the numbers were a jumble in his head. Mostly, he was imagining himself at the dance, looking as good as anyone.

So Dennis paid for his suit, got a ticket to pick it up when it was cuffed and ready, and then Gordon drove him home. He found his mom sitting in the living room, darning socks, and Dad was out in the garage again. Dennis was suddenly thrust back into his own world. He explained to his mom what he had done, leaving out the part about the shoes. She would know sooner or later, but he was too ashamed for now to mention the total figure he had spent.

"I think you did fine," Mom finally told him. "That's a little more than I hoped you would have to spend, but you chose quality. I'm sure you'll wear a suit like that for many years." She laughed. "If you'll just stop growing."

But she was clearly making the best of the situation. Dennis knew she was worried.

"I'm working a lot during the holidays, Mom. I'll pay you back right away. I checked in my savings book, and I have seventeen in savings, not fifteen, so that will help a little." But Dennis knew he had let himself get carried away. He still had to find a way to buy her a nice Christmas present.

"We'll make it work," Mom said. She slid a lightbulb inside a sock to give a proper shape to the heel, then began to compare threads so she could repair a hole. After a time she said, "I talked to Marjean today." Marjean was

a friend of hers from Wyoming who also lived in Ogden now.

"How's she doing?" Dennis asked her, though his mind was still on other things.

"She's fine. She gets more news from our friends in Afton than I ever do."

Dennis could tell that Mom wanted to tell him something and was working her way toward it. "So, what's going on up there?"

"Do you remember me telling you about a boy named Gerald Parker?"

"Uh . . . I'm not sure. I don't think so."

"He was my boyfriend in high school, I guess you would say. But Marjean was telling me today that Cathryn, his wife, died. She was only forty-two, but she had cancer. When they found what she had, it was already too late. She died right away."

"Wow. That's awful young to die."

"I know. And she left five kids, all still at home. Poor Gerald must be heartbroken."

"Tell me this," Dennis said. "How come you didn't marry him?"

Mom looked across the room, away from Dennis's eyes. "Oh. Well. Things happen. Gerald got a scholarship over to the University of Wyoming. He was a year older

than I was, and we always talked about my going over too, but I wasn't smart enough to get a scholarship, and my parents couldn't afford to send me."

"So did he meet a girl at the university?"

"No, he didn't." She stopped sewing and lowered the stocking to her lap. "When Gerald came home—for Christmas, or during the summers—he never asked me out anymore. He married a girl from Thayne, just a few miles up the road from Afton."

"Was that hard for you?"

"Well . . ." She seemed to consider how she wanted to answer, but then she said, "Oh, Dennis, it was the hardest thing I ever faced. I cried and cried."

"You were still in love with him?"

She may have nodded just a little, but she didn't answer.

"So when did Dad come along?"

"He'd always been around. He was working at a gas station by then. When I graduated from high school, I got a job at a store in town, and I would bump into him here and there. He started taking me to dances and things. Then he asked me to marry him."

"What happened to that Gerald guy?"

"He came back and got a job as a teacher and finally ended up as the superintendent of schools. But he never

once told me why he lost interest in me. Maybe it was just because we'd grown up together and I wasn't very exciting to him anymore."

"I'll bet you were prettier than the girl he married."

She laughed. "To be honest, I was. Quite a lot prettier." It was not the sort of thing Dennis would ever have expected her to say. "So it was something else he liked better about her," she added. "I guess I'll never know what."

"You still have some feelings for him, don't you?"

She raised her head slowly and finally looked at Dennis. "I guess I do. I guess I always will—doesn't a girl always remember her first love? But your dad and I have had a good life together."

Dennis knew she would never admit anything more than she already had. Still, she had wanted to say something about this to someone, and she hadn't chosen Marjean. She had chosen him. "Gerald made a big mistake," he told his mom.

"Well, that was a long time ago. And I have you kids. I guess everything worked out for the best."

Dennis thought he understood a lot of things about his mother that he hadn't realized before. It hurt him to think of what she had gone through—was still going through. Somehow, he still had to get her a dress as nice as the suit she had just helped him to buy.

CHAPTER 5

The Christmas dance turned out better than Dennis ever could have expected. On the night before the dance, Mom had taught him the steps to the fox-trot. But as it turned out, Judy Kay taught him much more. Early in the evening, he was counting the steps in his head, vaguely aware that his back was too stiff. Mom had told him to bend his knees a little and relax, but he was too nervous to manage that. With Judy Kay in his arms, however, he gradually began to feel more comfortable. She looked up at him and chatted at first, and her blue eyes and pretty smile made him forget most everything else. She began to move closer to him, too, and then, right while the band was playing "The Nearness of You," she let her head gently touch his cheek. It had never occurred to him how wonderful hair could smell. Before long, the two had blended to the point that he could feel the beat

of the music without thinking about it, as though it were the beat of their hearts.

Everything seemed perfect, sort of dreamy, to Dennis. The Boys' Association—probably with the help of a lot of girls—had decorated a big Christmas tree in the center of the gym, and they had strung red and green crepe paper from side to side to create a false ceiling. The band was made up of mostly older men, but they were good, and they played all the songs that were popular: "In the Mood," "Sentimental Journey," "White Christmas," and "Have Yourself a Merry Little Christmas."

Dennis and Judy Kay were double-dating with Judy Kay's friend Patty Doxey and her boyfriend, a guy named Drew Tanner. The two couples traded dances a couple of times, and they danced with a few other people, but mostly Dennis kept Judy Kay for himself. They did eventually stop to get some punch and little green holly-leaf cookies. Dennis had worried about finding things to talk about, but Judy Kay made that easy. The two took their refreshments and found a seat, actually the front bench of the gym bleachers, far from the band, so they could hear each other.

"Dennis, what do you plan to do with your life?" Judy Kay asked him.

"Well, I'm not exactly sure. I do want to go to

college. But it's hard to think very far ahead right now. The next thing I'll be doing is going to war."

"I'm proud of you for that. I'm glad that's what you want to do." Judy Kay turned a little toward Dennis, and her knee pressed against his. "I want to do something *interesting* with my life," she said. "Don't you?"

"I guess so. What do you have in mind?"

"I'm not sure. But if the war lasts, I want to join the WACS or the WAVES, maybe go overseas somewhere, maybe learn to fly an airplane or—"

"Oh, sure. Like they're going to let girls do that."

Her eyes popped wide open. "Dennis, women in the Army Air Corps fly airplanes. Didn't you know that? And they train men to fly. Some of 'em even teach men how to shoot antiaircraft guns."

Dennis tried not to laugh. "I'm sorry, Judy Kay, but I can't see you blasting German planes out of the air—or even teaching guys how to do it."

"I know. It's hard for me to picture it, too. But girls are doing *everything* now. It's not like the olden days. All you boys will be going off to the war before long, and I don't want to just sit at home."

"But we join up so we can protect our moms and our sisters. I don't want you to get caught up in a war. You're too nice for that."

"You're sweet, Dennis. But if you get a chance to shoot a Jap plane or knock out a German tank, aren't you going to do it?"

"Sure I am. But that's what guys do. It's expected of us."

She slid back from him a little and looked into his eyes. She was wearing a silky dress—she called the color "burgundy"—and she had her hair curled more elaborately than usual and held up by a ribbon the color of her dress. She looked older than she did at school, and, right now, more serious. "We have to win this war, Dennis, and I want to help. Is there anything wrong with that?"

Dennis had a hard time thinking of her trading in her beautiful dress for a pilot's uniform, but he could see how sincere she was. "Judy Kay," he said, "let me do my share *and yours*. Let me pay the price so you won't have to."

She slid close to him again and took hold of his arm. "You're so brave," she said. "When are you going to enlist?"

"I've already made up my mind about that. On the day I turn seventeen I'm joining the army. I want to be a paratrooper, the same as my brother."

"I can just see you in a jump suit. You'll be soooo handsome."

"I don't know about that. But I want to be in a crack outfit and fight alongside the best of the best."

"That's exactly right. But don't count me out. I can't join as young as you can, but I want to do *something*. You'll be my example." She looked into his eyes so admiringly, Dennis felt as though he already had that jump suit on, was already a hero. But then she seemed to realize something. "Dennis, when's your birthday?"

"October."

"You'll be leaving next fall?"

"Yup. A guy can sign up at seventeen as long as his dad signs with him."

Her eyes had turned soft. "Oh, Dennis, I'm going to miss you *so much*."

Dennis thought his heart was seizing up. He had never felt so manly in his life.

"I'll write to you, okay? And every day I'll look forward to the day you come home."

Dennis had always heard about love hitting a guy over the head, but he had never really believed in anything like that. And yet, here he was in the Ogden High gymnasium, his eyes locked to Judy Kay's, and love was expanding his chest like air in a balloon.

So they danced some more, and before the night ended, a singer crooned, "I'll Be Seeing You." It was a

song about a boy seeing his girl in "all the old familiar places," but as the lyrics continued, the idea was that the boy was not really seeing his girl; he was only remembering their times together. The final words were, "I'll be looking at the moon, but I'll be seeing you." Dennis pictured the poor soldier "seeing" his girlfriend even though she was far away from him.

By then Dennis was there with that soldier, off in some foreign land, defending his country and at the same time dreaming of the girl he had left behind. And no question, the girl was Judy Kay with her beautiful smile. He liked that she was spunky, that she wanted to join the army or the navy, but what he liked best was that she would wait for him, miss him, and she would be there when he returned.

And yet . . . in the back of his mind was a sense that he wasn't being quite honest with Judy Kay. He felt the way he had in that nice men's store—as though he were pretending to be something he wasn't. No question, he wanted to be a paratrooper, but he had thought a lot about the things Mr. Littlefield had said. Maybe most soldiers really were scared; maybe he wouldn't be so brave when the bullets were flying. He had made himself sound like Superman, but what would Judy Kay think of him if he lost his nerve in battle? In junior high, in gym class, a

guy had once wanted to fight him and had put his fists up, ready. Dennis had made a lame excuse and walked away. All the boys had laughed at him. Maybe that was who he really was.

Dennis tried to push the thought aside, just enjoy that final dance, but afterwards, he had something new to worry about. Drew drove to the Ben Lomond Hotel downtown. Drew had asked Dennis where he thought they should go to eat. Dennis had had no idea; he had told Drew, "I'll leave it up to you." But he was sure that the dining room at the Ben Lomond was very expensive. Another chunk of his money would be disappearing. When Drew ordered a steak, Dennis did too—so he wouldn't look cheap—and he told Judy Kay to do the same. But Dennis's share of the bill came to more than six dollars. He had never imagined that two people could eat up six dollars' worth of food in one sitting.

These money concerns were running around in Dennis's head as Drew drove to Judy Kay's house, but he liked that Judy Kay cuddled up close to him and then held his hand as they walked to her doorstep. What he didn't know was how this good-night thing was supposed to go. When he stepped onto her porch, he told himself he didn't have to kiss her yet; he would have plenty more

chances. Mom had told him to treat Judy Kay like a princess, to be a gentleman.

"Well, good night," he said. "I had a great time."

Judy Kay turned and faced him. She looked up into his eyes, and he was almost sure she wanted him to kiss her. He made a slight move to do so, but her head turned at the same time, and he took that to mean she was pulling back. Almost immediately, however, he realized she had been turning her face to help him out. Still, he had missed his chance, so he stepped back.

"It was a swell night," he said, even though he had already told her that.

And then Judy Kay said, "Aren't you going to kiss me?"

Dennis instantly felt his face burn. "Uh . . . it's only our first date," he said.

"But we've known each other *forever.*"

That was all the justification Dennis needed. The problem was, he didn't know how to get back to where they had been. And yet, there she was, moving up to him, lifting her head. Their lips touched, and Dennis realized he had never experienced perfection until that moment. He had kissed a couple of girls in elementary school, playing kiss tag. But this was entirely different. Her lips were pliant and warm. He had his arms around her, and

she was pressed against him. He felt a tingle run all the way through him. If he hadn't been in love before that moment, he had definitely arrived there by the time he stepped away from her.

"Thank you," he sort of gasped, and that made her laugh.

As he walked away, she said, "Hey, Dennis, you turned out to be a good dancer—and a good kisser, too."

He wanted to explain to her that everything he knew about kissing, he had learned in the last thirty seconds, but he had pretty much lost his power of speech.

Drew drove Dennis home before he took Patty to her house. Those two probably wanted to park somewhere for a while and neck. That was fine with Dennis. He just wanted to get home, lie on his bed, and savor the sensation that was clinging to his lips. He wanted to think about Judy Kay and not go to sleep all night.

But when Drew dropped him off at his house, Dennis noticed that the living-room lights were on. For a moment, he worried that Mom might be upset with his coming in after midnight. But he had told her he might be late, and she had assured him that she understood.

When he stepped inside, he saw his mom sitting on the couch alone. He started to apologize for being

late, but then he saw that she had been crying, and he stopped. "What's wrong, Mom?"

"Oh, nothing. I'm fine now."

Dennis took a breath. He had thought first of Glen, but now he was pretty sure he knew what had happened. "Did you have a fight with Dad?"

"Well . . . yes."

"Was it about my suit?"

"Dennis, don't worry about that. You know how he is. He never thinks we have enough money for anything."

"I shouldn't have bought such a nice suit."

"I'm glad you did. He'll get over it. In fact, when I told him about you paying for a lot of it yourself, he calmed down. Everything upsets him right now. He's worried. The paper said tonight that the 101st got pulled out of Holland, but it didn't say where they're going next. He's afraid that they might be getting ready to parachute into Germany."

Dennis took a long breath. The thought of Glen invading Germany was frightening to him. He had always known that this was coming, but no question, a lot of soldiers were going to die when they penetrated the German homeland. "I just wish we would get a letter," he said. "Why do you think Glen hasn't written?"

"I don't know, honey. It's what I'm worried about, too, and it's what's upsetting your father."

There was silence after that. Dennis wondered whether the big push into Germany would start before Christmas. He couldn't think of anything worse than to have to worry about that during the holidays.

"Honey, I didn't wait up because of any of that. I waited up to see how the dance went—and now I've ruined the whole night for you."

"No, you haven't ruined anything. It was nice. Thanks to you, I even danced okay."

"And what about Judy Kay? Do you like her?"

"Sure. She's a nice girl."

Mom smiled. "Your words say 'she's nice,' but that little gleam in your eye says you've fallen for her."

"Oh, sure. Mom, it was our first date."

"I know. But there it is, still in your eye. You really like her, don't you?" She touched his arm, and Dennis could see that she was pleased.

"I told you, I like her just fine."

"Did you kiss her?"

"Mom!"

"Well, did you?"

"On our first date?"

"I would have guessed that you wouldn't when you

walked out the door tonight, but I'm still seeing that smile you can't hold back. I think you did."

"Well, I'm not saying. But I'll tell you this much: if I did, it was her idea, not mine."

Mom laughed too loudly, and then she covered her mouth and muffled the sound. "Well, I'll just say this. Every girl who looked at you tonight was jealous of Judy Kay."

"That's the dumbest thing I've ever heard." But Dennis knew he was smiling again, as hard as he tried not to.

"I think that suit was the best buy we ever made. It was worth it, just to see the look on your face right now." She smiled. "And the shoes were worth it too—I guess."

Dennis had been very embarrassed when he had brought the shoes home. He decided not to tell her how much the dinner had cost—and how short he was on money now.

CHAPTER 6

Glen was using his entrenching tool—the shovel he carried on his pack—to chop at the frozen ground. He was in Belgium now, and his squad was setting up a perimeter on the edge of a pinewoods. His platoon leader had told the men, "Dig in deep. If we get shelled, these trees will scatter shrapnel everywhere, and limbs will turn into spears."

But it was late at night by the time the troops had arrived, and the digging was going so slowly that Glen worried it could take the rest of the night.

A lot had happened in the last three weeks. On the day after Thanksgiving, Glen's unit had been trucked out of Holland to a camp called Mourmelon, in northern France. They were promised badly needed R&R, but the officers had soon begun preparing the troops for another airdrop—and this time, everyone figured, the drop zone

would be located in Germany. Glen could feel the anxiety building among the troops. They were drinking harder and getting into more fights.

The men were allowed passes to nearby Reims or even to Paris, and most took advantage of that, but Glen was tired to the bone. More than anything, he wanted sleep. A cot wasn't exactly a "bed," and the weather was cold; still, he had been issued a heavy quilt. He felt more comfort than he had known in many months. He fell asleep instantly each night, just as he had hoped he would.

But then the dreams would always start again.

He would feel himself being swallowed in mud, and he would hear shells thumping into the earth, exploding, spraying debris, shaking the ground, and always, he would see Walsh's head, the splattering blood. Sometimes he awoke screaming, and men had to tell him to be quiet. And he was not the only one who was struggling.

Private Dibbs did use a weekend pass to go to Reims. He came back talking about the cathedral and the other sights to see, so Glen decided he would put in for a pass. But then a new order came. On December 17 the men of the 101st were awakened in the night and told to pack their gear. They would be moving out early in the morning. "This ain't no jump," the first sergeant bellowed

through the barracks. "We're going on trucks—somewhere north. I guess that means Belgium."

It could also mean they were heading back to Holland. What worried Glen—and everyone else—was that they were moving out in winter and they had no heavy coats, no winter gear. They grumbled through the remainder of the night, but they were packed up and ready to go before morning. They caught what sleep they could and waited—waited all day. "It's the army," Dibbs told Glen. "Hurry up and wait. Every time."

It had been dark again before the men boarded the trucks, and by then they knew a little more. German troops had counterattacked across the Rhine into Belgium's Ardennes Forest. They had attacked with the advantage of surprise and with a huge force of men, tanks, and air support. It was obviously a last-ditch attempt for Germany to reverse the progress of the war. Allied troops had been emplaced rather thinly in the Ardennes, and now every unit held in reserve was being sent in as quickly as possible. The airborne units—82nd and 101st—had been camped just outside Belgium, so they were going in as reinforcements even though they weren't infantry soldiers.

The men were jostled and bounced over rough roads and late that night finally dropped off near a town called

Bastogne. By then the roads were clogged by retreating Americans. "Bunch of cowards, if you ask me," Dibbs told Glen. And Glen thought so too. Some of these guys who were running from the battle had dropped their weapons. The 101st was known as the "Screaming Eagles," and the men thought of themselves as true warriors. They were trained to drop into the middle of a war zone and fight surrounded. Glen understood the temptation to panic, to run, but he also knew that it was something he could never allow himself to do.

The soldiers in Glen's company worried that they had little ammunition, and no one seemed to know where ammo dumps were located. Some of the retreating soldiers gave them M-1 rifle clips, and everyone shared what they had. But the airborne companies simply weren't equipped for a battle.

Glen was glad to be off the truck and moving his muscles. He warmed now as he walked. His unit eventually located more ammunition, but they still had nothing warmer to wear than light trench coats, and no one had winter underwear. They marched on through Bastogne—which was mainly one long, L-shaped street—and headed into the woods northeast of town, where they had received the order to dig their foxholes. At least there was

no mud or rain to deal with, but the hard earth was a new challenge.

After a time, Glen broke through the frozen top layer of the ground and started to make faster progress. Dibbs was digging next to him and hadn't been saying much, but he finally asked, "How much deeper do you think we need to go?"

"Who knows?" Glen said. "Those guys hightailing it out of here seemed to think the Krauts were right behind 'em."

"Yeah, but we've seen what happens. About the time we get dug in, the captain will move our whole company again and we'll have to start all over."

It really did seem to be what happened. Glen had sometimes wondered whether officers weren't trained to keep men busy—with any task they could think up—just so they couldn't sit around and complain to each other. But Glen also knew that when he heard incoming shells, he always wished he had dug deeper. "Listen, I can't sleep now anyway," he said. "Why don't you sack out on the ground, if you can get warm enough, and I'll keep digging."

"Naw. I don't want to be out on the ground if anything happens."

So they kept digging through much of the night

and finally tried to sleep a little. And then, before eight o'clock the next morning, Lieutenant Greene, the platoon leader, walked the perimeter and told the men they were moving out. Glen could hear soldiers all up and down the line grumbling, cursing, telling each other that they had known this would happen.

The troops marched farther northeast to another woods, this one looking down on a little town called Foy. It was strange for Glen to drop his pack and gaze across a tranquil valley, not green now, but full of grassy hillsides, cows gathered around little barns, houses with red-tile roofs. It all looked peaceful and safe.

Dibbs stood for a time taking in the scene, and then he said, "I wonder what's going to happen here." The two were obviously thinking the same thing: blood should never be spilled across a valley like this. And yet, Glen knew better. The clash of men and arms was near at hand.

The troops dug in again, the work taking much of the day. They also cut limbs and boughs from the nearby Scotch pines. They placed them near the foxhole, ready to be pulled over the top as a shield at night or whenever shelling began. The cover would hold a little body warmth inside the hole, and it would protect them to

some degree if mortar and artillery fire shattered trees and sent limbs flying.

But no attack came that night or the day after that. Glen wondered whether the Germans had been thrown back. This was not like the situation they had faced in Holland, where opposing troops could see one another with field glasses. It was colder here, though, and clouds were low and gray. On the third day snow began to fall. That night was a little warmer, but the snow only added to the difficulty of keeping weapons dry, and supplies were still not arriving.

Rumors had begun to spread from headquarters to the men on the line. Soldiers were saying that Bastogne was a crossroads on the edge of the hill country of the Ardennes. Most of the roads converged and split off in or near the town, like the spokes of a wheel. That's why the army had sent the bulk of the paratroopers to this crucial site. But the other news—again, according to rumor—was that the Germans had skirted the city, apparently aware that it was reinforced, and now Bastogne was surrounded. With the low clouds, there was no Allied air cover—and also no supply drops. And with no supply lines, coats and heavy underwear were not coming. Even rations were short.

Sergeant Caruthers, Glen's squad leader, had been

moving about, checking on his men. He told Glen and Dibbs, "Make your K-rations last. There's no telling when we'll get more."

After Caruthers walked away, Dibbs turned to Glen and said, "Someone, somewhere, must be thinking up this nightmare. How does the 101st end up in every mess that comes along?"

Glen had been thinking something like that, but he didn't say the rest. He had been praying so long that he could get through the war, make it home to his family, and manage to keep his head straight, but every time he gained a little hope that he would be okay after all, some new development made things worse. He didn't know what to pray for anymore. When he asked God to help him, he hated what that implied. He didn't want to think that God was in charge of the war, that He might protect one soldier and let another die. Walsh had been as religious as Glen. In Normandy he had gone into every church he could find, and he always knelt and prayed. No doubt he had prayed that he might survive, the same as everyone else did. Germans were surely asking too. Maybe the best thing for Glen was to put his life on the line and not ask for special favors.

The problem was, Glen had way too much time to think. The quiet was unnerving, and the cold simply

never let up. It was like an ache from the inside out. For most of the hours of the day, he and Dibbs stayed in their foxhole, where it might have been slightly warmer than out in the breeze, but it was also darker.

And then the attack finally came. Late in the night Glen heard the whistle of an artillery shell. He knew the sound and was instantly awake. A shell hit somewhere in the woods. It was not close, but more were already coming. For an hour the earth rumbled and rolled as though a volcano were stirring under them and spitting fire overhead. The sound of the explosions rolled through the forest, always closer, and finally the concussions tore through the trees like wind, sucking the breath from his lungs. Glen tried to make himself small in the bottom of his hole, tried to control himself as the terror built inside him. And then a shell hit close, and Glen heard shrapnel buzzing through the air, punching into trees and into the ground around them.

Glen lay as flat as he could and gripped his hands over his helmet. Dibbs was next to him, the two of them like spoons fitting together. Glen didn't know where his own shaking ended and Dibbs's began. But they didn't speak to each other. They just waited, heard the buzzing whistle of the shells, and then braced themselves as the thunder roared and the explosions flashed at the same

instant. At some point Glen thought he heard a scream, but the noise from the shelling filled the hole, the air, everything. For all he knew he might have been the one screaming, or maybe it had been Dibbs.

Glen did pray. He begged for help. And when a pause in the barrage set in, he waited. He was relieved that he was still alive, as always, but he hoped he hadn't embarrassed himself. He wondered whether he had prayed out loud. He hoped he hadn't prayed only for himself.

"Don't get up," Dibbs said.

He didn't have to explain. They both had been around long enough to know that the German artillery officers liked to stop, let soldiers start to move around to assist the wounded, and then let go with another attack.

But this time the calm continued, and Glen had a chance to realize that he was still cold, that he still had to get through the night. He needed to sleep if he possibly could.

Then the bombardment returned, more intense than before. The air turned to fire, and the explosions became a constant rage. The foxhole seemed to toss about, and each close strike shook through Glen's body. Something hit him like a hammer blow, knocking his helmet askew.

He didn't know what had happened. He only knew

that his head was ringing with pain. "Help me," he said. "Help me." Not to Dibbs, but to God.

The pounding of shells stopped as suddenly as it had begun, and when it did, Dibbs rolled over so that he was facing Glen. "Are you hit?" he asked.

Glen reached to touch his head, but his hand struck something protruding into the foxhole.

"It was a tree limb," Dibbs said. "Did it get you?"

"It hit my helmet."

Neither could see anything, but Dibbs grabbed the tree limb and pushed it up and out of the hole, and then he ran his fingers over Glen's head and face. They couldn't really see each other. "I don't feel any blood," he said. "I think it came through far enough to bang against your helmet, but that's all."

Glen took a long breath. Death had reached close enough to touch him, but not to take him. No matter the questions he had asked himself earlier, he prayed again, and this time he thanked God. It didn't matter what he understood or what he didn't. He felt blessed.

Glen and Dibbs waited. They both knew the shelling could start again. But after a time they pushed back enough limbs to look out. The clouds were slightly illuminated. The sun was coming up.

"We were lucky," Dibbs said. "That limb could have stabbed either one of us."

"It hit me in a good place. In the head," Glen said. But they didn't laugh.

Glen and Dibbs kept watching the valley beyond the woods. Sometimes a barrage like the one they had just survived was to batter and weaken troops before a ground attack. At least for now, though, all was silent. Dibbs finally said, "That salvo was as bad as we've seen. I don't think I've ever been that scared."

Glen was relieved that Dibbs would admit to it. "Humans have to stop doing this stuff," he said.

"Sure they do," Dibbs said. "But when's that going to happen?"

Glen found it disheartening to think that people couldn't learn, never would, that wars would never end. He thought of his little brother. Dennis should never go to war. He shouldn't ever experience any of this. He had to write to Dennis and tell him not to sign up. In his last letter, Dennis had said that he planned to enlist as soon as he turned seventeen, but he was still a kid. He shouldn't join up until he had to.

The clouds were gradually emitting more light. "Maybe we ought to check on the other men, Corporal Hayes," Dibbs said. "It's light enough to see now."

"All right. You go to the right and I'll check to our left."

Glen found some shaken men, but no one had been hit. He hurried back to his own foxhole. Dibbs was longer getting back, and when he returned, he looked pale. His hands were shaking. "Garner and Brooks got hit," he said.

"How bad?"

"Don't go over there. There's nothing left of them."

Glen didn't want to think about that. He had known Garner and Brooks from the beginning, from jump school days. He couldn't think why they had died and he had lived. He tried to force his mind to another place, and as he did, an image came to him. It was something he had remembered many times during the war. One day when he was in high school, he had walked past his parents' bedroom and glanced in. His mom had been kneeling by the bed, praying. It was in the middle of the afternoon, and Glen had had no idea why she had taken that time to pray. But now he often thought that she probably knelt and prayed multiple times each day. It just seemed what she would do. He didn't want to think; he just wanted to remember his mother praying for him.

He stared down at the peaceful valley, the little town of Foy, the rooftops so shrouded in fog that they were

barely discernible. All the artillery and tanks and mortars were somewhere farther off, but they were real, and
the peace in front of him was the illusion. He felt in his
pocket to see whether the sprig of lavender was still there,
but he felt only dust. He brought his fingertips to his
nose. He was almost sure that he still smelled the aroma
of lavender.

CHAPTER 7

A letter finally came from Glen. It was just a little V-mail that didn't offer much writing space, but the good news was, Glen had been pulled back to France for some rest. He was away from the action. That good news lasted only a couple of days, however, and then the radio and newspapers reported that the Germans had attacked across the Rhine into Belgium and had created a bulge in the front lines. The alarming part of the story was that the 82nd and 101st Airborne Divisions had been drawn into the battle and had taken up a defensive position near the town of Bastogne.

That was bad enough, but just before Christmas, news came that Bastogne was surrounded by German forces and in danger of being overrun. Dennis and his mom heard the story on the radio, and then Dennis read it in the *Ogden Standard-Examiner*. When Dad came in

from work, Linda and Sharon were close by, so Dennis waited until they had gone off to their bedroom before he read the news out loud to Dad.

When Dennis was finished reading, Dad said, "I heard all that on the radio today, and I'm mad enough to shoot somebody. It don't make sense to send those boys right back into the battle before they had a chance to rest some more."

It was what Dad always did: he got mad when he didn't like something.

Mom said, "From what the man on the radio said, they had no choice. No other troops were close enough to get there fast."

"Yeah, well, I'll tell you what, Norma. I don't believe what I hear on the news. They just tell us what they want us to know."

"I guess you're probably right."

"What do you mean, you guess? Maybe once in a while, I know what I'm talking about."

"I know you do."

At least Dad let the matter go. Dennis was relieved. He didn't want a fight to start now. He was too preoccupied, too scared. Glen was in a bigger mess than ever. He could be *overrun*. How would that turn out? Maybe he

would be taken as a POW. The trouble was, paratroopers didn't give up. They would never surrender.

"Why don't we have a prayer?" Mom said.

Dad nodded.

"Should I say it?"

He nodded again.

So Mom prayed that Glen's life would be preserved again, that he could keep his courage up and use wisdom. "Lord, it's almost Christmas," she said in her prayer. "Grant our son comfort. Let him know that we are praying for him, that we love him with all our hearts. Please, bring him home to us someday."

She was crying by then. Dennis was trying not to. Dad was silent. It was Friday, and Christmas was on Monday. But what kind of Christmas would it be?

Dennis had talked to Judy Kay about going to a movie that night, but he couldn't bring himself to go. He called her and told her what was happening, and how he thought he'd better stay home that night. "Oh, Dennis, they're playing *Christmas Holiday*, with Deanna Durbin and Gene Kelly. It would take your mind off everything."

Dennis thought of Gene Kelly dancing around. He just wasn't in the mood to see that. "I better not," he said.

"But I told Patty we would go with her and Drew."

"I'm sorry, Judy Kay. Everyone around here is just . . . well, you can imagine."

"Dennis, I do understand. But your brother is a *paratrooper*. I'll bet he's ready for whatever comes."

"I know. But he's surrounded and it's almost Christmas. I just . . ." Dennis couldn't finish. His voice had gotten shaky, and he didn't want Judy Kay to hear that.

"Yeah, that is hard," Judy Kay finally said. "Maybe we can go some other night."

"Okay. We'll do that." Dennis was starting to understand Judy Kay. Her heart was in the right place, but the war was like a movie to her. The good guys always won. But then, she didn't have a brother in the war.

Dennis knew he couldn't dwell on the worst possible outcome all the time. He needed to do what he could to salvage Christmas. He had gotten paid that afternoon, so he could pay Mom some more of what he owed her, but that left him only about ten dollars for Christmas shopping. He needed to buy a little something for his sisters and for Dad. If he could get gifts for about a dollar each, that would leave him with seven dollars, plus the five Dad had given him. He had gone shopping a few times during his lunch breaks the last couple of weeks, and he knew he could get a dress for twelve dollars, but

it wouldn't be nearly as nice as the suit Mom had bought for him. He thought of asking Dad for a few more dollars, but he was sure that would only bring on another tirade, so he let that idea go. He would just have to do his best with the money he had.

On the following evening, when he got off work, he walked to Kress's and bought new coloring books and a box of Crayolas for each of the girls, and he found a leather belt for Dad. Dennis had noticed that Dad's old belt was falling apart.

So Dennis had his twelve dollars, but he also had an idea. He couldn't stop thinking about that pretty dress in the window at L. R. Samuels. He had stopped to look at it almost every day, and nothing he had seen anywhere else was half as pretty. He was sure it would cost too much, but he wondered whether he couldn't pay the twelve dollars down and pay the rest after Christmas. So instead of heading toward Penney's, he turned the opposite way and walked back to take one more look in Samuels's window.

It was a cold night, but he stood outside the store for quite some time. All he could think was that he wanted his mom to have that dress. Just once in her life, he wanted her to have something that was so nice she would never think to buy it for herself.

Light snow had begun to fall. People were walking by, laughing and talking, saying "Merry Christmas" to friends. Garlands were strung across the wide street, and from somewhere Dennis could hear Christmas music. But it was the inside of the store that impressed him. Everything was upscale and tasteful, and the shoppers were well dressed. It was all foreign to him—a world he didn't know.

He had on his wool school coat with the collar turned up and a stocking cap. The men inside were wearing topcoats and felt hats, and the women carried leather handbags and wore gloves, bright scarves, and showy hats. He didn't know if he dared to go in there looking the way he did, but he just kept imagining the look on his mom's face when she opened a gift box and found that dress inside.

So he walked in. He didn't know where to go, but at least no one seemed to notice that he didn't belong there. He stood by the front doors and looked around for dresses. Lifelike mannequins were perched on high stands, all of them dressed in pretty outfits. He walked down an aisle, turning sideways to get past people who were looking at clothing on the racks or talking to salesladies. And then he heard a soft voice say, "May I help you, sir?"

He didn't think she was talking to him. No one had ever called him "sir." But he looked around to see who had such a kindly voice. It was a woman who seemed about his mom's age. She was wearing a red dress, and she looked classy, with red lipstick and dark hair, dark eyebrows. If he hadn't heard her voice, he would have thought she was a little too hoity-toity, but she had sounded nice.

"Oh. Well . . . I saw a dress in the window. I was looking to see if I could find it. Or, you know, one like it."

"Which one was it?"

"That purplish one."

The woman smiled and nodded. "Isn't that a *lovely* dress?" she said. "I call it 'lavender blue.' You know, like the song."

There was a song he had heard on the radio, something about "lavender's blue, dilly, dilly." But he had no idea what that meant.

"I guess it's more lavender than blue," she said. "But the shade is just perfect. You may have noticed, this year the style is to wear pastels and pretty colors in winter. I think it's a way of saying, 'Maybe there's a war on, but we're not going to be gloomy.'"

"I like that idea." He thought of the lavender water his mom always wore. Maybe lavender was her color, too.

The woman was still smiling, but something in her eyes seemed sad. Not gloomy, just a little sad.

"I'm afraid it is quite expensive. How much were you thinking you could spend?"

Dennis didn't want to say. "I only have twelve dollars, but I thought maybe I could pay that much now and then pay the rest after the first of the year."

She was already shaking her head, but she looked disappointed. "I'm sorry, we can't take payments that way. We only do that on layaways. But with Christmas on Monday, it's too late to hold anything."

"Okay. I was just wondering." Now he wanted to get out of there. It had been foolish to walk into a place like Samuels and ask such a dumb question. He pulled off his stocking cap and stuck it in his pocket. He could just imagine what sort of guy she thought he was—with only twelve bucks in his pocket and thinking he could buy an expensive dress. "I better go down to Penney's," he muttered. "They have some dresses I can afford."

"Have you thought about getting your mother something else? Maybe a blouse or a sweater? We have some very pretty blouses for less than ten dollars."

"No, that's all right. She needs a dress for church."

"Well, that one would be perfect. The fabric is wonderful, but the dress itself is trim and simple." She

hesitated, and then she did something Dennis hadn't expected. She touched his arm, the way Mom always did, and she said, "I'm so impressed that a boy your age would want to do something special for his mother." Now he heard something new in her voice, not just kindness but a hint of the sadness he had seen in her eyes. The way she said it, he thought she must be a mom herself, and he didn't feel quite so stupid. Still, it was time to head to Penney's.

"Let's take a look down here," the woman said. "We do have some dresses in your price range." She took a couple of steps and then looked back. "Just push and shove to get through. That's what everyone else is doing."

She laughed and he smiled. She really was a nice lady.

"What's your name?" she asked.

"Dennis Hayes."

"Okay, Dennis, follow me. I'll push and you shove."

But she didn't really push; she just zigged and zagged a little. And people were actually being friendly—laughing and talking as though they liked being crowded. The place smelled nice, too, like cinnamon, and there was Christmas music playing: "I'll Be Home for Christmas." Every family seemed to have someone in the war who would actually *not* be home for Christmas. That was what the song was really about.

They reached some racks filled with dresses, and the saleslady asked him, "Dennis, do you know your mother's size?"

"I think it's six, or something like that. She's little."

"My size, maybe?"

"Kind of, but you're a little taller."

"Size six could be right. Let's look."

But every dress she pulled out seemed like something a woman would wear in an office. They were gray or brown, and the material in them seemed heavy, not shimmery like the one in the window. The woman kept holding dresses up next to her, spreading them over her red dress, and they all looked dull by comparison.

"Well . . . I don't know," he finally said. "I guess I'll just look around some more."

"Tell me this. What was it about the dress in the window that you liked so much? Was it the color, or . . . what?"

"Mostly, I guess."

"We don't have anything else in—"

"I mean, I liked the color, but mostly, it didn't look like anything my mom has ever had. I just thought she would like to wear something really . . . you know, *beautiful,* at least once in her life."

The woman looked at him for a long time—just

stood there in that crowd and looked into his eyes. "You're close to your mother, aren't you?"

He nodded.

"I think it's wonderful that you want to do something so nice for her."

"My dad gave me some of the money."

"So why did he send *you?*"

"He said I would know what she likes."

She nodded. And then she did it again—touched his arm. "If I held the dress for a little while," she said, "do you think you could run home and get more money from your father?"

"No. That's already more than he wanted me to spend."

"I understand. I'm so sorry I can't find anything you like as much. . . ." Her voice thickened and then stopped altogether.

"It's okay," Dennis told her. "I knew I probably couldn't afford it."

But he didn't walk away. He could see in her face that she wanted to say something else. "Are you your mother's only son, Dennis?" she asked.

"No. I have a big brother. He's in the army." And then he said more than he meant to. "He's in Belgium.

He's in that city they're talking about on the news. Bastogne."

She let out a little gasp. "The place that's surrounded by Germans?"

He nodded. Her eyes were suddenly moist. He knew that he needed to leave before he felt too much. "Well, thanks for helping me. I'm sure I can find something in another store."

He started to turn, but she said, "Wait." Then she didn't say anything for a moment. He could see that she was considering. "Here's a possibility, Dennis. I think the dress in the window would fit her. I'll have to check the size. But maybe our manager would discount it, since it's been on display. Maybe you could get it with the money you have."

Dennis didn't know what to think. She had said it sort of businesslike, but she was still blinking back her tears.

"Just wait right here a minute and I'll do some checking," she said, and then she hurried away.

So he stood in the aisle, conscious again of all the people around him. But he wasn't feeling quite so out of place. One woman even said "Merry Christmas" to him after she bumped into him.

The saleslady was gone a long time, and by then

Dennis was anxious to get going. He didn't think the dress could ever be discounted as much as he needed.

But when she came back, she was smiling. "It is the right size," she said. "And I worked things out with our manager. Just give me the twelve dollars, and it's yours. It's what we do with the dresses that have been in the window. I don't know why I didn't think of it sooner. Would you like to have me wrap it for you?"

"Oh, yeah. I'm not good at that."

So they zigged and zagged again to the back of the store, and she got out a box, folded the dress, placed it gently inside, and spread tissue paper over it. Then she wrapped the box in pretty red paper and added a gold ribbon. When she finally handed it over to him, she said, "Would you do something for me?"

"Sure."

"Would you stop by the store after Christmas and just tell me if your mother liked it?"

"Oh, sure. I can do that."

"Is your mom terribly worried about your brother?"

"Yeah, she is."

"And you are too, aren't you?"

He nodded.

"Do you pray for him?"

"About twenty times a day."

"I'll pray for him too. What's his name?"

"Glen."

"Glen. I like that. Will you also let me know how things turn out for him?"

"Sure. I can do that." He took a step away, and then he turned back. He nodded to her, tried to think of something really polite to say, but he only came up with, "Thanks. Really. Thanks so much. You didn't have to go to so much trouble for me. Merry Christmas."

She nodded, and then she came around the table. She touched his arm one more time. "I'm just glad I had a chance to meet you," she said. "And I'm happy we could work out a way for you to buy the dress you wanted."

Dennis wasn't quite sure what to make of his feelings. He only knew that he was fighting back tears, and he didn't want anyone to see that. But he did let go a little as he walked out the door. He was just so touched by the woman's kindness and concern, and he felt that a miracle had happened. There should have been no way for him to buy that dress for his mother, and yet it was tucked under his arm now, and Mom would have the Christmas gift he had longed to give her.

Dennis kept wiping his tears away, and he lowered his head when he passed people on the street, but the walking warmed him, and he was filled with gratitude.

God knew him, it seemed, and knew Glen, knew his mother—and cared about them all.

He wanted to cling to those feelings and never doubt again. But he knew himself. As much as he prayed, he still feared. He wanted to see his brother again, but it was hard to trust that that would ever happen. Dennis had also admitted something to himself in recent days. His seventeenth birthday was starting to feel close, and he realized that if he joined the army that fall, maybe neither he nor Glen would get home, and Mom and Dad would be left without their sons. He knew it was cowardly to worry about such things, but the thought wouldn't go away.

CHAPTER 8

The war news was the same on Sunday. Dennis tried to remember the comfort he had felt the night before, but it was hard not to wonder whether something might happen to Glen. After all, he was not just away at war; he was surrounded. And he was out in the cold. Even if everything turned out well in the end, Dennis could only think how lonely and maybe afraid his brother must be on Christmas Eve.

After the girls went to bed that night, Dennis could hear them giggling and talking. He kept wondering, if the worst news came about Glen, what would happen to them, to the family? Glen had always seemed to be the glue that held everyone together—the one they all loved. First son. Big brother. If he didn't make it home, maybe one of those fights between Mom and Dad would end with Dad leaving.

Dennis didn't go to bed until very late. He tried to read but couldn't concentrate. Finally he just lay on his bed, and eventually he did drift off. He woke up later and got under the covers. He was finally sleeping soundly when he heard Linda and Sharon squeal as they charged to the Christmas tree. Dennis got up, pulled on a pair of corduroys and a flannel shirt, and walked out to the living room, still barefoot. He saw his presents, the ones that weren't wrapped, lying on the couch by the tree. There were an Argyle sweater-vest and a white shirt and tie. It wasn't a lot, in a way, but it was too much, considering what Mom had already spent on him.

Everyone had placed gifts under the tree for one another, and there were presents from grandparents—sent from Wyoming. Mom told the kids not to open anything until Dad came out. So Linda and Sharon ran after him, screaming wildly and telling him to come out *"right now."*

Finally Dad came out dressed like Dennis—no shoes and an old shirt—and he had on some worn-out dress slacks. He hadn't shaved, and his thinning hair was tangled. But what Dennis noticed most was that he seemed lifeless, as though this whole Christmas morning business was some sort of ordeal he had to pass through. He walked straight to the couch and sat down. Then he looked at Mom and said, "All right. Go ahead."

Dennis knew what that did to Mom. She had tried so hard to make this morning as nice as possible for everyone.

Dennis said, "I'll tell you what, Mom, ol' Santa has me pegged. He knew *exactly* what I wanted." He laughed, tried to sound happy. He wanted the girls to have a real Christmas.

"Just a sweater and shirt?" Linda said. "You only wanted *clothes?*"

"Good-looking clothes."

Linda and Sharon both had Betsy Wetsy dolls. They wanted Mom to fill the little plastic bottles with water so they could feed them.

Dennis watched Mom. She must have gotten up really early, even before Linda and Sharon had made their charge. She had built a fire in the kitchen and had put on a flowered wraparound dress. It was just a housedress, but it was her best one, and she had combed her hair and put on lipstick. "Wait just a minute, girls," she said. "You have all day to play with those dolls. Let's open our other gifts, but let's do it one at a time, so we can all see what everyone got." That was what she said every year. "Dennis, you be Santa. Hand out the gifts one at a time."

Dennis knew how this was supposed to go. He always made sure every person received a gift before he

started on another round. It was what Glen had done when he had played Santa.

Dennis found a present for Dad first and handed it to him. "Here's something for you, Dad," he said. "It's from Mom."

"Go ahead and let the girls go first," Dad said.

"They'll get their turn. Open it."

So Dad pulled the ribbon and fumbled with everything until he got the paper torn off. What he found inside was the same thing Dennis had gotten: a white shirt and a maroon tie. He glanced at Mom, and Dennis could see that she was embarrassed. Maybe the hint was a little too obvious. It was like saying, "This is so you'll have something to wear to church—and I wish you would go." But Dad said, "That's very nice," and he set the box down next to him on the couch.

"This is for you, Mom," Dennis said. "It's from Sharon."

"Oh, my," Mom said. "I didn't know you got me anything, sweetheart." She acted excited—more, Dennis could tell, than she really was.

Sharon had made her gift at school. She had pressed her hand into clay, and then she had painted the hand-print gold and the clay around it baby-blue, with some sort of sparkly stuff in the paint. "This is *wonderful*,"

Mom told Sharon. "Really. I'll treasure it forever. When you're all grown up, I'll look at this and remember my sweet little girl."

"You'll have to think about both of us," Linda said. "I made exactly the same thing for you."

Mom laughed, and she knelt by the girls and hugged them both, kissed each on the cheek.

And so it went for a time, with books for the girls from Mom's parents—which Linda glanced at and pushed aside—and a set of Old Spice aftershave and cologne for Dennis, from the girls, but certainly chosen by Mom.

"Hubba, hubba," Linda said. "Judy Kay will get a whiff of you and give you smackers all over your face."

Sharon thought that was extraordinarily funny, and the two girls giggled and nodded and started directing noisy air smooches toward him.

Dennis kept going, handing everything out. Dad opened the package with his belt inside, nodded toward Dennis, and then set it aside with the white shirt. The girls pretended to be embarrassed when they each got underpants in their packages from Grandma Hayes, but they liked their new coloring books from Dennis.

Mom gathered up all the wrapping paper and ribbons, saved what she could, and expressed way too much

joy over hot pads and dish towels Grandma and Grandpa Hayes had sent her.

Dennis finally said, "Well, I guess that's everything."

Linda reacted the way he knew she would. "Nuh-uh," she said. "There's something else back in the back." She was sitting on the floor where she could see under the tree.

Dennis acted surprised, and then he crouched and looked. "Oh, yes, I do see a red package behind the tree. Let me see who that's for."

"You know what it is. You put it there," Sharon said. She was giggling again.

"It says, 'For Norma,' so it must be from Dad."

Mom actually did look surprised. She sat down next to Dad on the couch. She carefully untied the golden bow and unwrapped the red paper. Dennis heard her whisper, "L. R. Samuels?" She glanced at Dad.

Dennis was holding his breath, waiting, watching her face as she took the lid off the box.

Her eyes opened wider, and then he saw her confusion. She took another look at Dad, but he was staring at the dress, the same as she was, and he seemed just as baffled. She touched the fabric with her fingers, hesitated for a moment, and then she lifted the dress out of the box. She stood up and held it away from her by the shoulders and took a long look. "Oh, Hal, it's *beautiful*," she said.

He was still looking puzzled. "Dennis and I went in on it together," he finally said.

"Oh, Dennis, did you pick it out?"

Dennis nodded. "Did I get the right size?"

Mom draped the dress next to her, the way the lady at the store had done. "I think so," she said. "I'm going to go try it on." She held it out and looked at it again. "It's the prettiest dress I've ever seen. It's just perfect."

She reached down and took hold of Dennis's hand and pulled him up. She hugged him and thanked him, and all the while Dad was still sitting on the couch. Mom did turn and say, "Thank you so much, Hal. I just love it." But Dennis could see what all this was doing to him.

Mom disappeared down the hall and into her bedroom. Dennis finally got the nerve to look at Dad.

"Samuels?" Dad asked.

Dennis just looked at him. He didn't want to justify anything. He didn't want to talk about it. He just wanted Mom to be happy that she had something really nice.

Dennis knew he ought to be ashamed of himself for receiving so much of the gratitude from his mother, but the truth was, Dad wouldn't have done anything had Dennis not asked him for the money. And Dennis was still thinking of his mother's face when she opened the box. She had been happy, even today—in spite of everything.

After a few minutes, Mom came back with the dress on, and she was glowing. She twirled around in her bare feet, once slowly, and then twice more, more quickly. "It's so *elegant*," she said. "It glistens when I move. And the color—I never saw such a beautiful color."

"It's purple," Sharon said.

"Oh, but it's so much more than that. It's more lavender than purple, and it's like there's a blue light shining through it, or . . . I don't know. It's perfect, and look how it fits me."

She was looking at Dennis again, and now he didn't care if Dad was mad at him for paying so much. "The woman at the store said that ladies are wearing pretty colors this winter. It's like saying, 'War or no war, I won't be gloomy.'"

"That's exactly right," Mom said. "We have to count our blessings and hope for the best."

"You're *so pretty*, Mom," Sharon said. "Like a movie star."

"Oh, honey. Not really. But thank you for saying it." Her eyes, however, showed that she believed Sharon. She knew she was pretty. "I better take it off now. I'll wear it to church next Sunday." She looked at Dad, and she finally walked over and bent to kiss him. He didn't raise

his head, so she kissed him on the forehead. By then, she was obviously realizing that she had hurt him.

Dennis watched his mother shrink back into herself, so he got up and walked toward her. Then he stopped and stayed back a little. He didn't want her to hug him again. Dad had seen enough of that already. "Mom, it was Dad's gift to you. I just helped him pick it out."

"And I appreciate it so much, Hal," Mom said.

"I saw that dress and I knew it was meant for you," Dennis said. "But it was kind of a miracle that I was able to get it." He looked at his dad, even waited for him to look up. "It didn't cost nearly as much as you might think. The lady at the store gave me a really good deal."

Dad showed no response. He didn't say anything at all. Mom only nodded, and Dennis was sure that she didn't want to fuss over it anymore, didn't want to upset Dad. But when Dad got up and walked back to his and Mom's bedroom, Mom whispered to Dennis, "Thank you so much. It's the nicest gift I've ever received."

"I wanted you to have a dress that was as nice as the suit you helped me buy. I looked at other dresses, but that color seemed perfect for you. I couldn't stop thinking that I wanted you to have it."

Tears filled her eyes. "Thank you," she said. "I'll always remember that you did something so nice for me."

CHAPTER 9

Glen and Dibbs were huddled in their foxhole, where they had stayed most of the time the last few days. More than a foot of snow had fallen, and everything in sight was white and frozen. The nights lasted fourteen hours, and low clouds trapped a dull gloom over everything during the day. No supplies were getting through, so the men were still wearing their jump uniforms with trench coats. They still had no warm socks, long underwear, or gloves. Headquarters tried to send hot food to the line some days, but the meals were nearly as cold as everything else by the time they reached the troops.

On the morning of Christmas Eve, the Germans had struck hard in a sector just east of where Glen's company was camped. All day Glen had expected a barrage in his direction. He could hear tanks roaring in the snow only a few miles away, and mortar and machine-gun fire kept

breaking out, but the Germans, for now, weren't aiming any of their fire at Glen's company.

The sounds of the fight calmed in the afternoon, but the wind came up, and the cold became more intense. At least the fog and clouds blew away, and Allied fighters and bombers were able to strike at the German forces to the north and east. Reports had reached Glen and Dibbs that D Company of their battalion had been taking a beating. There had been heavy casualties, with no way to evacuate the dead and wounded. Glen hoped that the air attack might slow the German advances and open up supply lines into Bastogne.

Glen and Dibbs ate white beans and little else that evening. The dark came early again. As they huddled close to one another, with tree limbs and logs stacked over their heads, Glen felt the dark as much as the cold. He could still hear bombs dropping not far away.

"I hope our boys are giving it to the Krauts," Dibbs said.

Glen hoped so too. But he couldn't get it out of his head that it was Christmas Eve. A phrase came back to him—something he had said in a third-grade play called "Christmas Around the World": "The Christmas tree comes to us from Germany. German children leave their shoes outside their doors and wait for St. Nicholas to

place candy and gifts in them." That was pretty much all he had known about Germans until he had learned to hate them.

"I guess the bombs are our little Christmas gift to our Nazi friends," he told Dibbs. *"Frohe Weihnachten."*

Glen knew that it was best not to talk about Christmas, about home, about food, about comfort. But, of course, that was mostly what he and Dibbs did talk about. Now it was Dibbs who asked, "So is this what you usually did back in Utah on Christmas Eve? Eat white beans and sit in a dark hole all night?"

"No. But I like this so much, it's what I plan to do from now on."

They each laughed quietly, and then there was silence until Dibbs asked, seriously, "So, when do you open presents at your house?"

"Christmas morning."

"Yeah. We did too. But Mom would let us open one present on Christmas Eve. We'd get our whole family together that night. All my uncles and aunts and cousins, Grandma and Grandpa. We'd sing Christmas songs, and Grandpa would read the Christmas story from the Bible. And we'd always have a big supper. Then each of us got to open that one gift. I could never get to sleep that night,

I was so excited. I loved the whole thing. Every minute of it."

Glen thought of his mother busy with baking and getting everything ready for Christmas morning. Dad never let on as though he cared much about such things, but Glen knew better. He remembered the year when he was about seven and had wanted more than anything to get a bicycle for Christmas. He had told his parents, but Dad had seemed anything but receptive to the idea. "Hey, Santa's not made of money," he had told Glen. On Christmas morning, when Glen had gotten up and hadn't seen a bike, he had been crushed with disappointment. He had put up a brave front, accepting the shirts and books and underwear he had found by the tree and pretending he was fine with them. But Dad had been unusually lively that morning, and he finally said, "I thought I heard some bells jingling outside last night, Glen. You might want to check on the front porch and see whether Santa left anything out there." Glen had gone out and discovered the bicycle. That moment was still his favorite memory from his childhood.

So Glen let it all run through his mind again, the year of his red bike. When he had found that bike on the porch, he had noticed that it wasn't new. In his young mind, that proved that the gift had come from Dad, not

Santa—and that had made it even better. His dad could repair anything and make it work. Glen had always been proud of that, and proud that Dad could catch fish when no one else was getting a bite, and could shoot a running deer all the way across a canyon. Dad was a hard man in some ways, and too impatient, especially with Mom, but to Glen that surly, moody guy had never been the one he thought of as his father. The father he loved could take an old bike and make it new—and teach Glen how to hunt and fish.

Glen didn't tell Dibbs the story about the red bike. He just rehearsed it in his mind, and then he let his thoughts wander to summer days, riding with his friends in the neighborhood. He also remembered teaching Dennis to ride, and later passing the red bike on to him.

Bombs continued to fall, and Glen kept picturing the chaos and destruction someone out there was being forced to survive. Of course, he also knew some of them were not surviving.

Dibbs finally said what Glen had caught himself thinking. "It just seems wrong to kill on Christmas Eve."

"I know."

It wasn't good to think about that, and usually Glen didn't. What he knew, though, was that German soldiers, whether they considered themselves Nazis or not, were

hunkered down the same as he was, and each one was probably praying he would make it home to his family one day. What Glen also knew was that he might kill one of those German boys sometime soon. Or he might get killed by someone who loved Christmas as much as he did.

"War doesn't make sense," Glen whispered.

"I know. I was just wondering, what does God think of us?"

Glen let the question sink in, but it wasn't helping him. He knew he had to change the conversation. "The thing is, God's depending on us to stop Hitler."

"Sure. But I still think human beings have made a mess of this world—no matter how much hot air General McAuliffe likes to blow."

Earlier that day a letter from General McAuliffe had been carried to the front lines and distributed to the men. The letter—read in foxholes or shared out loud in camps—described the Germans sending an envoy with a message that American troops were surrounded and cut off. In his letter, the German general had offered American troops a chance to surrender. McAuliffe had sent back a one-word response: "Nuts!" And then, in his letter to the troops, he had pumped up the incident as something for the men to take pride in.

"The general's letter makes a better story if you're living in the center of Bastogne in a warm building," Glen said. "Maybe he needs to spend a night out here."

"That's what I was thinking. I'd like to get inside for ten minutes—just get warmed through *once* before we face another night out here. But he's still right. We aren't going to surrender. And I don't think we should."

"I know."

But the words didn't make Glen any warmer. He couldn't stop shivering. He felt as though ice had penetrated the cells of his body. His feet had lost all feeling, and he worried what that might mean. Each day he and Dibbs were supposed to pull off their boots and take turns rubbing each other's feet to keep their circulation going. But it was a painful, miserable process, and they hadn't done it that day. Glen wondered whether they would pay for that.

Eventually Glen and Dibbs sat down and covered over their foxhole. Then, as the cold penetrated deeper, they took up their sleeping position. The night seemed endless. The worst thing was, this night included two hours out of the foxhole and into a fortified dugout called an "observation post," where Glen and Dibbs had to watch and listen for German patrols. At night, patrols from both sides attempted to size up the enemy.

Opposing patrols would engage at times, fire off a few rounds, and usually retreat. Observation posts were also a likely target. At least their own sector stayed quiet that night, but the cold was worse out of the hole, and it was a relief to finally return to the foxhole and to lie sideways in the narrow space, each seeking body heat, unembarrassed to hold onto one another.

Glen had joined the army full of enthusiasm and courage, ready to do whatever he had to do to protect his country. He still believed he was doing that. But at the moment there was nothing to fight except this cold, and it was winning. The only future he could see was more and more days—and nights—like this. He wondered how much longer he could stand it. He was seeing the same thing in Dibbs's eyes now, in all the men. They were reaching another breaking point, even worse than what they had experienced in Holland.

Glen felt himself cascading into hopelessness, so he prayed. He didn't ask for victories or for much of anything except that the Lord might be with him, comfort him. When Glen had needed comfort in his life, it had always been his mother who was there to care for him. He wished now that God could send her to him, that she could hold him, warm him, take care of him the way she had done when he was sick sometimes as a little boy.

He tried to feel her presence, to imagine that she was there, and it seemed for a time that she was, that the sweet smell of her was all around him.

Then he awoke, and he realized he had actually slept, hadn't dreamed, hadn't seen Walsh, had managed to get some rest. The sun was shining, thin shafts coming through the limbs above him. He felt renewed, felt that God had heard him. And then he remembered: it was Christmas morning.

He had received a tender gift.

But bombs were falling again, and they fell all day. Glen decided that it was better to talk about running the Germans off than it was to talk anymore about Christmas. Still, he kept thinking of home, of seeing his family. He pictured Christmas morning, the tree, playing Santa. But the memories didn't hurt so much today—not after the blessing the night had brought and the sense he was still clinging to that his mother had been with him.

In the afternoon Glen and Dibbs took off their boots, rubbed each other's feet, and dried their socks as best they could by holding them against their skin, under their arms. They both felt better, warmer, when they pulled their boots back on.

News came that day that the Germans had been slowed by the Allied air attacks, and the battle that had

created a bulge in the line—and was already being called the "Battle of the Bulge"—seemed ready to take a turn for the better. Someone had heard that a supply line had been opened, and winter clothes would be coming soon, but nothing happened that day to prove the rumor true. Still, it seemed possible that better days might be ahead. All the talk was that the airborne troops would return to France to finish their training for their eventual drop into Germany. It was an ominous prospect, but the idea that their division could return to warm barracks and beds—or at least cots—was all Glen wanted to think about for now.

Then, on the afternoon of Christmas Day, mortar shells began to drop into the woods. For all the talk of victory, the Germans clearly weren't finished. Glen and Dibbs crouched in their foxhole once again, and the sound of exploding ordnance—not just mortars but tank fire and artillery—filled the air. The blasts shook through Glen's muscles and sucked the air from his chest. Trees were splitting apart, crashing, shrapnel scattering like random bullets, and the ground bounced as though they were in the middle of an earthquake. Glen was gasping, pulling his helmet down with both hands, hearing the noise as though the explosions were inside his own head. To Glen it seemed as though a vicious animal were on the

loose, clambering through the woods, bellowing, reaching for him.

Somewhere in the middle of all the noise, Glen thought he heard a scream. And then, with each pause in the chaos, he could hear, "Medic, medic." Eventually he heard an agonizing cry, as though from sorrow, not just pain. "Help us," a voice was pleading. "Help us."

Glen started to get up, but Dibbs grabbed him and pulled him down. "Not yet," he shouted. "Don't go out there."

But the shelling had stopped, and the voice was hysterical. "Medic! Medic! We're hit. We're both hit. Please, please, help us."

Glen jumped up. He pushed a limb off the top of the foxhole and scrambled out of the hole, but he didn't know where the sound had come from. There was snow everywhere, spattered with black patches of exploded earth, and there were dark pine limbs strewn in all directions. He watched, looked around, and then he heard the call again. "Medic! Please!"

The voice was much weaker, but Glen thought he knew the direction. He took three or four steps, heard it again, and then began to run.

Just then he heard the buzz of another shell, and almost instantly, a flash filled his vision. He felt the blow

to his body, felt debris slap into his torso, his legs. He was tumbling backward, dropping, twisting. The side of his face hit the snow and buried into it. "Mom," he said. "Mom." And then the light was gone.

CHAPTER 10

While Mom was changing out of her new dress on Christmas morning, the girls asked Dennis to help them fill their baby bottles. He still wanted them to have fun, so he joked with them, told them he was going to potty train the dolls instead, but he finally followed them to the kitchen and filled the bottles. Before long, Dad walked through the kitchen in his coveralls and work shoes. Without saying a word, he grabbed his coat and walked out the back door.

When Mom came out, she was wearing her house-dress again.

Dennis waited until the girls ran off to their room before he said, "Dad's mad, isn't he?"

"I guess so. He wouldn't talk to me. But that's not your fault."

"I didn't mean to show him up. I just wanted your Christmas to be happy."

"I'll talk to him. I'll tell him how much I like the dress—and how good it was of him to help pay for it."

"Yeah. Do that," Dennis said. "He'll be okay with it, don't you think?"

"Whether he is or not, it's the nicest Christmas gift I've ever received."

"Good. I just pray that Glen's all right. Then this day will be a good memory, not a sad one."

"Oh, Dennis, I pray all day, every day. But we'll have to accept whatever comes—and make up our minds to be happy—the way so many families have had to do."

Dennis knew exactly what she meant, and he knew she was right. Still, he was never going to stop praying for Glen.

"Dennis, you have a wonderful soul. You care so much about people. I don't know what I'd do without you."

Dennis was embarrassed. "Mom," he said, "I wish I was half as good as you think I am."

She laughed. "Don't argue with your mother. I'm the boss around here." She walked to the back door. "I need to get breakfast started." She opened the door, probably

to go out to the icebox on the back porch, but she looked back. "I guess your dad headed out to the garage."

"Yeah. Do you think he has a bottle out there?"

"I don't know. He might."

"Would it help if I talked to him? Maybe I need to tell him I'm sorry."

"Maybe it wouldn't hurt to say something to him, but you'll have to watch how you say it."

So Dennis got his shoes and coat on and walked outside. He found Dad at his workbench, fiddling with something. He turned to see who had come in, saw Dennis, and immediately turned back around. Dennis could see that this was going to be difficult.

"Dad, I should have told you that I got the dress at Samuels. But it had been on display in the window, so the woman gave it to me for a really good price."

"How much?"

"Twelve dollars."

"I only gave you five."

"I know. I put in a little more than I'd planned."

Dad walked to his stool. He pulled a pack of cigarettes and a lighter from a pocket in his coveralls. He lit a cigarette and sat down. Dennis was still standing across the garage from him. He felt awkward. He hated this

pitiful place: the messiness of everything, the smell of grease, the cigarette smoke.

"Why, Dennis? Where's she going to wear a fancy dress like that?"

"She can wear it to church."

"They'll laugh at her. They'll think she's showing off."

Dennis didn't think so. Most people would tell her how pretty she looked. Dad thought dressing up was a way of acting stuck-up, but not everyone looked at it that way.

"You never have figured out who we are, Dennis. Why should we buy things at stores that charge twice what you'd pay at other places? That's all just to pretend we're something we're not."

"It wasn't that. I just saw it in the window, and it was—"

"I'll tell you what you are, Dennis. You're ashamed of your own family." He took a draw on the cigarette and then slowly let the smoke seep from his nostrils. He stared at Dennis with a look that seemed part sorrow, part hatred. He was only forty-one, but he looked old to Dennis. His eyes looked pasty, almost yellow, and his skin gray. His hair was thin and light, and there were strands of white in it already.

Dennis didn't say anything. He wasn't ashamed of

his family. His feelings were a lot more complicated than that. But how was he supposed to explain that?

"You think you have to prove that you're not a big nobody like your dad."

"That's not true." But even as he said it, Dennis knew his dad's words were closer to the truth than not.

"You hate everything about me. I work with my hands. I wear coveralls. I've got grease under my fingernails. You've been going out with this girl, but you never bring her around here. You don't want her to see where we live. And you sure don't want her to meet me."

This time he had struck even closer to the heart of the matter. Dennis thought of trying another denial, but he knew he wouldn't be convincing.

"I'll tell you something else. Your mother feels exactly the same way about me. She wishes I could work in a bank—like her brother up in Afton—and wear a suit and tie to work. Well, guess what? She's stuck with me, and she better settle for what she's got—or I'll just walk away one of these days."

"That would break her heart, Dad. She doesn't want that. And I don't either."

"I don't believe that, Dennis. You and your mother have each other—always cooking up your little plans to improve me. Don't think I don't know that."

There was nothing else to say. Dennis knew he wasn't going to convince his dad of anything. But he never had been good at keeping his mouth shut. "Why don't you come back in the house," he said. "It's Christmas. Mom's making breakfast. Why stay out here?"

"I'll come back in when I'm ready. You're the one who needs to head back to the house."

"Just don't drink, okay?"

He knew the moment it left his mouth that it was the worst thing he could have said. Dad stood up and pointed his finger at Dennis. "Is that what your mother sent you out here to tell me?"

"No. It's what scared *me*. I know what happens when you come out here and drink."

"What happens, Dennis? Tell me."

"You get mad. You come back in the house and fight with Mom. And—"

"And you take *her* side."

Dennis tried to sound as neutral, even gentle, as he could. "Dad, you aren't yourself when you drink. You say mean things to Mom. I think if you heard a recording of yourself after you're sober again, you'd regret the things you say."

Dad stood stiff and crossed his arms across his chest, still holding the cigarette. "Or maybe there's another

way to look at it. Maybe I spend my life bowing down to your mother and to you kids, and I finally say what I really think—and what's true—when I've had a couple of drinks."

"I've seen you grab her sometimes, Dad. And you double up your fist. I'm afraid you're going to get drunk and hit her one of these times."

"Have I ever hit her?"

"Not yet."

"That's right. And I've been mad enough to knock her down. But I never have, and I never will."

"Last time you drank, you told Mom that she doesn't care about you. But I watch her work her head off to put your favorite meals on the table. She washes your clothes, keeps the house just perfect, and she—"

"That's what a housewife does."

That was almost more than Dennis could take. He wanted to charge his dad, knock him on his back.

"I go to work every day, Dennis. That's what I'm supposed to do. And she keeps house, and she does very good at it. But that doesn't mean she cares about me. She loves you kids, but if I walked out tomorrow, I'm not sure she'd miss anything but my paycheck."

Dennis was way too angry. "When you happen to get one," he yelled.

Dad dropped his cigarette on the floor and took two quick steps toward Dennis. But then he stopped himself. He stood with his fists doubled, his jaw set. "Get out of here," he said, his voice hard as a hammer.

"I'm sorry, Dad. I didn't mean that. You work hard, and you can't help it that your work slows down sometimes."

"Get out of here."

Dennis knew he had made things worse, and he was sure that if Dad had any whiskey stuck away, he would get it out now. "Dad," he said, "I'm sorry I said that. But you need to know, Mom always tells me how much she appreciates all you do for us. When I get mad at you, she tells me I shouldn't, that I should recognize what a good man you are. Don't take it out on her just because I said the wrong thing. She's so worried about Glen. She doesn't need anything else to worry about today."

Dad didn't move. He was still staring at Dennis, but these last words seemed to reach him. He took a breath, let it flow out, and then he said, "I'll tell you something about Glen. He's a smart kid, and a good kid, and he'll probably do something good with his life. But he'll never look down on me. He thinks I'm a pretty good guy—his *dad*. I'm okay in his eyes even if I take a drink once in a while. It's you and your mother who think I'm a drunk

and a dirty little car mechanic. And I'm sure the girls are starting to think that way too. So I just hope that Glen makes it home. Maybe me and him can hunt and fish together. Every time I ever took you anywhere, you acted like you wanted to get away from me just as fast as you could."

Now Dennis was the one staring, thinking. "It always seems the other way to me," he said. "It seems like you don't like me."

Dad put his hands on his hips, looked down at the floor. "I guess I don't, Dennis. You might be right about that. But it didn't start out that way. It didn't have to get to that point."

Dennis felt as though he had been sliced open. He had told himself that his dad hated him, but he had never quite believed it. He hesitated for a few seconds, but there really wasn't anything else to say. He turned to go back to the house.

As Dennis put his hand on the doorknob, Dad said, "Wait a minute."

Dennis turned around. He could see a change in his dad's face, but what Dad said surprised Dennis. "I haven't had a drink since Thanksgiving. Have you noticed that?"

"I'm not sure. Yeah, I guess so."

"Well, I haven't. I'm trying to quit drinking, whether you believe it or not."

Dennis nodded. "That's good," he said. He waited.

Dad stared at the floor for quite some time. Finally, without looking up, he said, "I shouldn't have said what I just did. I'm sorry."

"It's true though, isn't it? You don't like me."

"Sometimes I don't. You make me feel like I'm nothin' more than trash. Your mother does the same thing. I have a hard time with that."

Dennis knew he had to be honest, and yet he had to say something that would not break everything apart between them. He took a couple of steps forward, but he didn't dare cut the distance any more than that. "Dad," he said, "I'm starting to think straight. My friends used to talk about their dads being businessmen and lawyers, and I guess I wanted you to be like that. But that's not the right attitude, and I know it."

"It is in one way, Dennis. You're smart. I want you to go to college. You should be a doctor or something like that yourself. But I've seen what's coming for a long time. You'll make a lot of money, buy a fancy house—all those things. And then you'll think you're too important to come by this little place. All your life you'll look down

on your old man—who never could make anything out of himself."

"That's not true, Dad. You can do all kinds of things I'll never be able to do. Your hands bothered me when I was a little kid. I'll admit that. But they shouldn't. They just prove that you aren't afraid to work."

"A guy who can fix things for other people doesn't get paid a decent living, Dennis. Rich guys come into the shop, flash a little money, and say, 'Get my Lincoln running for me.' But they don't respect me. They never will. That's just the way the world is. That's why you think of me the way you do."

"But it's the wrong attitude."

"Maybe so. But I'm always going to live in one world, and you're going to live in another. Your kids are going to laugh at Grandpa with the grease stains on his hands."

"No. I promise I won't let my kids think that way."

"Well . . . we'll see." He slipped his hands into the pockets of his coveralls. He looked down at the floor again. All the anger was gone from him now. "Go back in the house. I'll be in in a few minutes."

They both stood for a time, and finally Dennis dredged up what he had always wanted to say. "Dad, you don't like to touch me. Even when I was little, you didn't

like me to sit on your lap. You shake my hand once in a while, but that's about it."

"I know." He was still looking at the floor. "That's just how I am, Dennis. That's how my dad was, and that's how I've turned out to be. But I don't know how to be any other way."

"Okay. I understand."

They looked into each other's eyes for a moment, and then Dennis nodded.

"I'll come in before long."

"Okay." But the two were too close to a resolution. They needed to get there. "Dad, when Glen comes home, maybe the three of us could go fishing again. He might even get home in time to go deer hunting next fall."

"Yeah. I'd like that. I hope he's home by then."

"If he doesn't make it home . . ." Suddenly all the emotion Dennis had been holding back came pouring out. His voice broke; tears ran down his cheeks. He took a deep breath, waited for a time, and then he started over. "If he doesn't come home, maybe the two of us could go fishing in the spring, or we could hunt in the fall, before I enlist."

Dad was blinking, swallowing. Dennis had never seen him like that. "We can do that," he said. "That would be good."

"Okay."

"But Dennis, you're not enlisting in the fall—not at seventeen. Your mother couldn't stand it if you and Glen were both gone." Dennis heard the strain in Dad's voice when he added, "And I don't want that either."

Dennis wanted to walk toward his dad. Even more, he wanted his dad to come to him. But he knew that wouldn't happen. So he said, "Well, come in for breakfast."

"Okay. I'll be in in a minute."

Dennis nodded, and then he went back to the house. He was a little scared, though he didn't know exactly why, but at the same time, he felt as though he was a different person now, and always would be.

CHAPTER 11

Dennis was working full-day shifts at Walgreen's during the after-Christmas sale. He still owed his mom some money, so he was glad for the work.

On Friday morning Dennis was getting ready to go to work. Linda and Sharon were coloring at the kitchen table and listening to a program on the radio. Mom had said she wanted to check on Mrs. McClean, who had been sick since before Christmas. "What time are you leaving?" she had asked Dennis, and he had told her nine-thirty. "I may not make it back quite that soon," she'd said, "but the girls will be all right for a few minutes." And then she had reminded Linda and Sharon about some chores they had been putting off: dusting and sweeping and cleaning up their room.

After Mom left, Sharon had walked to the little closet off the kitchen and found a broom, but Linda told her,

"Don't sweep the floor. There's nothing to sweep. Just tell Mom you did it. She'll never know the difference." Dennis knew how much Linda loved to tell Sharon things like that, just to put her in a quandary.

"Linda, I can't—"

"Okay, okay. Just sweep it really fast, but the floor's not dirty, if you ask me."

Just as Dennis was telling Sharon to do a good job and not listen to Linda, a knock came at the front door. He couldn't think who would show up at their house at this time in the morning, but he walked through the living room and opened the door. When he did, his body instantly jolted. He didn't reach for the screen door, didn't say anything. He stared. The boy on the other side of the screen nodded, as if to say, "Sorry," and then said, "I have a telegram for Mr. and Mrs. Henry Hayes."

He was just a kid, maybe thirteen, but he was wearing one of those Western Union hats, flat on top, and everyone knew what that meant. No one ever wanted to see those boys.

Dennis still didn't open the screen door. Everything was a jumble in his mind.

"Is either one at home?"

Dennis shook his head.

"Are you their son?"

He nodded.

"You can accept the telegram," the boy said. And then he was the one who pulled the screen door open. He was suddenly in focus, the rusty screen no longer between them, and he was extending the telegram toward Dennis, who was thinking that he shouldn't take it. It seemed that it couldn't hurt him if he never read it. But he already felt sick.

Dennis took the telegram, even signed for it, but then the boy walked away and Dennis still stood there with the door open. He couldn't think what to do. He knew he couldn't open it, but he wasn't sure whether he should go to his mom. She would want to read it at home, not at Mrs. McClean's. Or would she want Dad to be with her? He just didn't know.

About then he saw Mom hurrying down the street. He waited in the doorway.

Before she reached the porch, she was saying, "Gloria saw a boy stop here—a Western Union . . ."

Dennis was nodding. He held the envelope out to her.

She came in and took it from him, but she didn't open it. Dennis had never seen her so pale. She sat on the couch and looked again at the envelope, but she didn't open it.

"Linda, Sharon," Dennis said, "turn the radio off."

"Why? We're listening to—"

"I said turn the radio off."

He sounded, even to himself, like Dad. The radio clicked off, and the girls appeared in the living-room doorway. He saw the fear take over their faces. They knew about telegrams too.

Mom looked at them, and then at Dennis, and she said softly, "We have to be brave about this. We can't go to pieces. We have to accept God's will, and we have to honor Glen's courage."

Dennis nodded, but he was feeling destroyed.

In spite of her words, Mom had begun to sob. Still, she worked her fingernail under the flap of the envelope and pulled out the little sheet of paper. She looked at it carefully. And then, in a gasp, she said, "He's not dead. Wounded."

Dennis hadn't known the War Department sent telegrams for wounds. He took a long breath. He nodded a couple of times, and then he asked, "How bad?"

"I don't know." She handed the telegram to him. It read: "REGRET TO INFORM YOU YOUR SON CORPORAL GLEN HAYES WAS WOUNDED IN ACTION IN BELGIUM STOP YOU WILL BE

ADVISED AS REPORTS OF CONDITION ARE RECEIVED."

"What's 'wounded'?" Sharon asked.

"He got shot," Linda told her.

"Not necessarily," Dennis said. "It could be . . . lots of things." And then he looked at Mom. "Maybe he's not hurt too bad."

"I know," she said.

But of course, Dennis knew the possibilities. Glen might be on his deathbed, for all they knew. Or already dead. Maybe his legs had been blown off. Or he was blind or mutilated. Dennis had seen all those things, knew of boys who had come home on crutches with a leg gone, or men with burned faces.

"I've got to telephone your dad," Mom said. She took a deep breath. "But now we'll have to wait again."

It was what they had been doing for so long, and yet this seemed worse than ever to Dennis.

"He's my little boy," Mom said. She began to sob again. "Someone has hurt him, and I can't even take care of him."

Dennis dropped to his knees in front of her and grabbed her hands. She leaned forward and pressed her face against the top of his head, and then she cried for a long time.

"We'll just keep praying," Dennis said. But he didn't feel much faith in that. The Lord, it seemed, would do as He chose, regardless of what Dennis asked. Mom wanted him to accept, and he knew that was what he should do, but right now he felt more anger than acceptance. All he could think was that God should have struck Hitler down Himself, not expected so many young men to sacrifice themselves to stop the man.

Dennis was late getting to work, but he went. He told his mother that he would stay home with her, but she said, "And do what, Dennis? We can't just sit here. We can't just cry. We'll hope for the best, and we'll go about our business."

She was pulling herself together again, preparing to accept whatever came next. Dennis had calmed a little by then, and he knew that he had to do the same thing.

"Dennis, we've always known he might get hurt." She wiped the tears from her face with the palm of her hand. "Or killed. We're no different from anyone else. And look how many others have lost their sons."

Dennis knew that, too. He told his mother, "I think he'll be all right." The problem was, he saw in her eyes, and knew inside himself, he had only said the words because they sounded good.

Dennis left as Mom was picking up the phone to

break the news to Dad. He walked down the hill to work, and he went straight to Mr. Littlefield to explain. "I'm sorry I'm a little late," he said. "We got a telegram this morning. Glen's been wounded."

"Oh, dear. How bad is he hurt?"

"We don't know."

Mr. Littlefield put his hand on Dennis's shoulder. "Well, remember what I told you. This might be the wound that brings him home."

Dennis had been thinking the same thing, but he didn't like Mr. Littlefield saying it. The man thought soldiers all wanted to get away from the war. Maybe some did. Maybe most did. But Glen wasn't like that.

So Dennis didn't say much more. The sale was over, and end-of-the-year inventory had begun. He went to work counting items, listing them, and he tried to think only of that. And then, a little before lunchtime, Judy Kay and Patty came into the store. Dennis didn't want to talk to them. He knelt and counted things that were on a bottom shelf. But before long he heard Patty's big voice, like a boy's. "Young man, could you help us, please? We're searching for water from the fountain of youth and we heard you sell it in bottles out of your back room."

He looked up, tried to act as though he hadn't seen them coming. He didn't want to talk about Glen, didn't

want them to know how upset he was. "We do have that product, ma'am," he said, "but we don't waste it on the young. Could you come back in fifty years?" He tried to laugh and didn't do very well.

Patty said, "That's not fair. We're young and beautiful now, and we want to stay that way." She patted her hair as though she were primping for a photograph.

Dennis stood up and tried to think of something he could say. He finally came up with, "I do have some black salve right here. It's good for corns, bunions, snakebites, deep slivers, mosquito bites—almost anything, really. I put it on my pimples."

The girls laughed a little harder than the joke deserved, and then Patty said, "Oh, but we never have pimples. We have perfect skin. Haven't you noticed?"

Dennis just couldn't keep the banter going. "You both look great. No doubt about that," he said, but his voice sounded serious.

Judy Kay seemed to sense something. "I heard that our troops broke through to that town where your brother is. Do you think he'll be okay now?"

There was no way Dennis could avoid answering. "Well . . . no. We found out he got wounded. We don't know how bad."

Now everyone was silent.

"We got a telegram this morning."

"And it just said 'wounded'?"

"Yeah."

"But you're worried, aren't you?"

"Sure."

Judy Kay stepped a little closer. "I'm sorry," she said.

Patty took a step away, as though she thought Dennis and Judy Kay might want to talk. But Dennis only said, "Maybe they'll send him home." He tried not to show much emotion.

"But that's the last thing our boys want," Judy Kay said. "They want to be patched up so they can get back to the action. Some of them go back over and over. They keep fighting no matter what."

"I guess. If they can."

"Dennis, your brother is a hero. He's saving our nation. That's what you have to remember. Even if he has to lay down his life, he'll do it. For our freedom."

"Yeah, I know. That's right."

"And next year you'll be out there with him. If you aren't fighting the Krauts, you'll be going after Japs. I'm just so proud of you, Dennis. There'll be no stopping you, once you get over there."

"I don't know about that. I'm not . . . anything to be afraid of."

"Just wait until you're fighting for America. You'll show what you've got inside."

Dennis couldn't think what to say. He had a feeling Judy Kay didn't really know much about him. Maybe it was time he warned her that he may not satisfy her expectations. "My dad doesn't want me to go this fall. I don't think he'll sign with me."

"I don't understand. Why wouldn't he?"

"I'm not exactly sure."

"You can talk him into it, can't you?"

"Maybe. But if my brother doesn't make it, I don't see how I could go off so soon. I don't know what that would do to my mother."

Judy Kay was stopped. She stared at Dennis for a few seconds. "Dennis, lots of mothers have sent more than one son to the war. Your mother is stronger than you think she is. She'll do what she has to do."

"But she might need a little more time."

Judy Kay's eyes pinched tight. Dennis could see how disturbed she was—or maybe just baffled. "Dennis, I hope you're not the one who wants more time. Don't blame it on your mother if you're the one who's scared to go."

Dennis thought maybe Judy Kay was right about him, but he didn't say so. "No. I'll go," he said. "I'm not

saying that I won't. I'm just saying, I might not go quite as soon as I thought."

"I don't understand this, Dennis. You sound like a momma's boy."

Judy Kay wasn't smiling, wasn't flirting, and it occurred to him that she wasn't so pretty as he had once thought. So he said what was on his mind: "War's just a story to you."

"What?"

"Soldiers kill people, Judy Kay. And soldiers die. Or some get crippled for life."

"Do you think I don't know that?"

"No. You don't know it. You just think you do."

She placed her hands on her hips and stared into Dennis's face. "I'm thinking I don't want to go to the Valentine's Dance with you after all," she said, as if that were the hardest punch she could think to throw at him.

"That's okay. I don't blame you. I actually don't think I'm the kind of guy you're looking for."

"You're exactly right about that."

"You're a nice girl, Judy Kay, but you only know words. You can't see anything—or *feel* anything. I don't know if you ever will."

She flushed red, stammered, and then she cast a few more insults at him before she turned and grabbed Patty's

arm. The two walked away. Dennis was actually relieved to see them go. But, he told himself, he would go to war. He *would* fight for America. He just wouldn't pretend that dying was something grand and glorious. If Glen died, Dennis knew he and his family would never be the same, and he would never turn his brother's death into one of those sappy, star-spangled endings he had seen in the movies.

CHAPTER 12

By the time Dennis's lunch break came, he was glad to get away from the drugstore and out into the cold. But as he walked up the street, he didn't know where to go. Mom usually packed a sandwich in a lunch pail that he carried to work, but that morning he hadn't wanted to bother her about that. He finally decided he would walk into the Kress's five-and-dime and spend a nickel on a candy bar, just to hold him over.

Inside the store, though, he smelled the food at the lunch counter and stopped long enough to look at the price of a grilled cheese sandwich. It cost twenty-five cents—thirty-five with French fries—and that was more than he wanted to spend, so he turned to walk away. Just then he heard a woman's voice. "Dennis, I was hoping I would run into you one of these days."

It was the woman from L. R. Samuels. He hadn't noticed her sitting at the counter. "Oh," he said. "Hello."

"You promised to come back and tell me how your mom liked the dress."

"I'm sorry. I've been planning to do that."

"I don't think I ever told you my name. It's Louise Clifford."

"Oh. Nice to meet you. I mean . . . to see you again."

She held out her hand, and he shook it, but he felt funny about that. She was wearing a black coat with a red scarf, and she had on that bright red lipstick he remembered. She looked like the rich ladies who shopped at her store.

"So tell me. What did your mother think of the dress?"

"She liked it."

"What about the color? Was she all right with that?"

"Oh, yeah. She thought it was really pretty."

"Well, I'm happy it worked out for her."

"Yeah . . . really . . . it was great. Thanks so much for figuring out a way that I could buy it."

Mrs. Clifford had pivoted on the counter stool so she was looking toward Dennis. He was looking at her but also seeing himself in the mirror in the background. He noticed that there was no real joy in his face; he hoped

she wasn't picking up on that. He tried a little harder. "She told me it was the best Christmas gift she'd ever received."

"Oh, good. I'm so glad to hear that. What about your brother? Have you heard anything from him?"

"Well . . . yes." Dennis stepped a little closer. He didn't want everyone at the lunch counter to hear what he was going to say. "He got shot—or wounded some way. We got a telegram this morning. But we don't know where he is or how bad he was hurt."

The words seemed to stab her. He could see the color leave her face. "Oh, dear. How's your mom doing?"

"She's worried."

"I can imagine. And you're worried too, aren't you?"

"Sure." But he wasn't going to let the gentleness of her voice play on his emotions again. He turned a little and tried not to look at her. "Well, I'm glad I happened to come in here today," he said. "I really was going to stop by your store one of these first days."

"Sit down for a minute, Dennis. Are you on your lunch break?"

"Yeah."

"Let me buy you a hamburger or something. Would you like that?"

"Oh, no. I'm fine."

"Please. Join me. I'd like to talk to you a little more."

Dennis really didn't want to do that, but he couldn't think of an excuse to walk away. He sat down on the stool next to her. He felt strange when he looked in the mirror again and saw the two of them next to each other. He wondered whether everyone at the counter was trying to figure out why someone like him would be sitting next to such a dressed-up lady.

A woman in a pink waitress dress was walking toward them. She pulled a pencil out of her hair. "Hi, Louise," she said, and then she nodded to Dennis and waited. Mrs. Clifford said, "The same for me as always, Winnie. But bring a hamburger and French fries for Dennis. And a malt. What flavor, Dennis?"

"I don't need a malt. I wasn't going to have lunch."

"What flavor?"

"Strawberry, I guess."

Winnie nodded and wrote it down. "Are we in for a big storm?"

It took Dennis a couple of seconds to realize she was asking him. "I don't think so," he said. "A few flakes are falling, but I don't think we'll get hit too hard."

"I hope you're right," she said. "My tires is bare as a baby's bum. I'll never make it home if it snows hard."

She walked away before he could respond.

Mrs. Clifford was smiling. "No one has decent tires these days. It's a wonder the world doesn't stop when snow comes."

"I guess that's why I walk everywhere."

"Do you live close to town, Dennis?"

"Sort of." He didn't want to say exactly where.

She turned toward him a little, but he continued to watch her in the mirror and not look directly into her face. "Tell me about your mother," she said. "I remember you said you're close to her."

"Yeah, I am. But there's not a whole lot to tell. She's . . . just . . . regular. She stays home mostly."

"Did she grow up here?"

"No. She grew up in Afton, Wyoming, up in Star Valley."

"Is your dad from there too?"

"Yeah. He and Mom moved down here when I was a little kid."

"What does he do?"

"He's just, you know, a car mechanic. But he does better down here than he could up in Wyoming."

"What do you mean *just* a mechanic?"

"Well . . . I don't know."

"Dennis, don't ever say that about him. He provides for your family, doesn't he?"

Dennis nodded. He thought of what Dad had told him about being ashamed of his house, his family. He knew he shouldn't have answered that way. "Yeah, he does."

"And what about your brother? What will he do when he comes home?"

Dennis was glad she didn't say "*if* he comes home." He answered, "I don't know. Mom always says she wants him to go to college. She says the government will pay for it now that he's been a soldier."

"That's right. He can get money through the G.I. Bill. But is that what he wants to do?"

"I think so. He's kind of like Dad. He can fix things. And build things. But he got good grades in school, too. And everyone likes him. Mom thinks he could be a good salesman. She says he has the 'gift of gab.'"

All that was hard for Dennis to say. The telegram that morning had changed everything. Maybe Glen wouldn't be himself—if he got back.

After a time Winnie came back with the food. She came strutting up with Dennis's sandwich and malt on one platter and a bowl of soup and a slice of white bread on another. She set everything down, and then she dug some utensils out of a little apron she wore around her

middle. "There's napkins right there," she said, pointing to a napkin holder as she walked away.

Dennis and Mrs. Clifford started to eat, and for a time they didn't say anything. Dennis could hear all the little noises at the counter, cups clicking against saucers, the mumble of people talking. He thought he noticed people glancing at him in the mirror; that only added to his self-consciousness. He wanted to put ketchup and mustard on his hamburger. He saw only ketchup, but he didn't bother Winnie or get up and walk to where there might have been mustard on the counter. He just settled for the ketchup.

"Dennis, Glen might be fine. You know that, don't you?"

"Yeah, I do." Dennis could hardly believe that she had remembered Glen's name.

"But if he's not, you'll have to be strong for your mother. You'll be *everything* to her then. So let her know, she can tell you when she's scared."

"She's the one who's brave, Mrs. Clifford. She told me and my sisters, we have to accept what comes and not go all to pieces."

"She's right, of course, but you need to know, she'll battle back and forth with that. She'll say those things, but sometimes she won't really feel them."

Dennis thought he was understanding something about Mrs. Clifford. "I guess that's right," he said. Then he added, "I've been reading in the paper that the Germans are retreating now. Maybe the war will end before he gets sent back to the front." It was what Dennis had started to hope for.

"But Dennis, even if the war ends in Europe, I don't think the Japanese will surrender until we invade their islands. You can imagine how long that could take."

"I know. I worry that doctors will patch him up just in time to ship him to the Pacific."

"That could happen. Or he could be crippled by his wound. Whatever happens, you'll have to be strong, and you'll have to stand by your mother. Is your dad a good support to her?"

Dennis considered saying that he was, but Mrs. Clifford was being straightforward with him. He didn't want to lie to her. "Not exactly," he told her. "He's worried about Glen too, but he doesn't . . . say things."

Mrs. Clifford nodded, as though she had somehow guessed that. "Help her, Dennis. Let her cry. Let her be angry if that's what she feels. But don't tell her what she ought to feel."

"All right."

"I've been praying for your mom and brother, but

Dennis, I've been praying for you, too. I only met you for those few minutes in the store, but I saw how much you loved your mother, and that touched me. I want you to know, I've been praying that the war will end before *you* have to go. Your mother shouldn't have to send another son."

Dennis thought about telling her that he wanted to do his part. But he didn't say it. In fact, he told her what he had been thinking lately. "Mrs. Clifford, I'm worried about leaving her. My dad's been pretty good lately, but sometimes he drinks, and he gets mad at her. If we lose Glen, I don't know what might happen to all of us. I'm afraid . . . I don't know. Maybe he would get too angry sometime and hurt her, or maybe he'd just leave, and Mom would have the little girls and . . ."

Dennis wasn't sure how to explain it all. He didn't know what might happen if he were gone, but the one thing he had been sure of for a long time was that he had to look out for his mother. Maybe Dad knew that too. Maybe that was why he had told Dennis he wouldn't sign with him when he turned seventeen.

"Dennis, you're carrying way too much of a burden for a boy your age."

Dennis gritted his teeth, tried not to feel anything. But suddenly he was saying what he hadn't planned to

say to anyone. "I've worried a lot lately, Mrs. Clifford. I'm afraid what might happen to Mom and Dad, but I'm afraid of the war, too. I used to think I'd be a good soldier, but I'm not so sure anymore. I think maybe there's something wrong with me."

"Why do you say that?"

"Lately, I try to imagine myself killing someone, and I don't want to do it." Dennis was looking at the mirror, not at Mrs. Clifford, but he was seeing everything through his own tears. He ducked his head. "When I try to picture it, I think, *The guy—my enemy—has a mom at home, and maybe brothers and sisters, and they're all praying for him the same as my family prays for me.*"

Dennis hunched down, pulled his neck into his coat, and wiped his face quickly with his fingers. He tried with all his power not to make a fool of himself in front of that mirror.

"Oh, Dennis," Mrs. Clifford said. She slid her arm around his shoulders. "What's wrong with our world? Why do we have to teach boys to kill?"

"We have to win this war. I have to do my part."

"I know. I know. But it's still too much to ask of you—of anyone."

The waitress was coming their way. She stopped in

front of Dennis, obviously concerned. "You okay?" she asked.

"He's fine," Mrs. Clifford said. "He's just a little too good for this world, Winnie. Just as he ought to be."

Dennis was looking at the counter, not at Winnie, but he heard her ask, "Was he a friend of your son's?"

"No. Dennis and I are friends. We met at the store."

Suddenly, it was all clear.

"Well, I hope everything's okay," Winnie said.

"Yes. He's fine."

Winnie walked away. Mrs. Clifford let some time pass before she said, "Dennis, we had a son. Gary. He was a pilot. He was killed last June, flying paratroopers into Normandy on D-Day."

"My brother was one of those paratroopers."

"Yes."

"They could have known each other."

"Well . . . that's not very likely. There were so many."

Dennis understood that, but he envisioned them together, two young men going off to war. One had died, and, so far, the other had lived. Other things were also falling into place in his mind: clues he should have picked up on that night he first met Mrs. Clifford. All at once he knew for sure what he had only suspected that night. "The dress," he said. "You bought it for me, didn't you?"

"No, Dennis." She hesitated. "I mean, I did pay some of it. But don't ever tell your mother that. She should always remember that it was from you."

"And Dad."

"Well, yes."

Dennis wiped his eyes again. He knew he had to stop acting like a little kid. He had to get hold of himself.

"When you came in that night," Mrs. Clifford said, "you reminded me of Gary. Not your looks, but just the way you talked—and the nice things you said about your mother. I understood what your mom was going through, and I knew why you wanted to help her get through it; I just wanted to help a little." She turned on her stool so she faced the counter, the mirror. "I was feeling sorry for myself, Dennis—you know, because it was my first Christmas without Gary. What I needed more than anything was to think of someone else. It was good for me to give your mother a little lift, but it was a lift for me, too."

"I appreciate it so much, Mrs. Clifford. It made Christmas happy—better than it should have been. I wish you could have seen my mom. My sisters said she looked like a movie star, and she twirled around and around, like she really was one."

"It does my heart so much good to hear that." There

were tears in Mrs. Clifford's voice. She pulled a handkerchief from her coat pocket and dabbed at her eyes. Then she cleared her throat and said, "I'd like to ask something from *you* now."

"Okay."

"I want to see your mom in that dress someday. Will you come to our house—maybe some Sunday for dinner—and have her wear it?"

"I guess. I can ask her."

"I want so much to be her friend. And there's something else I would like."

"All right."

"I have no grandchildren, Dennis. There were complications when I had Gary. I couldn't have babies after that, so he was our only child. But I want you to do something for me. I hope it doesn't sound too strange to you."

"I'll do it, whatever it is."

"Okay. Here's what I'd like. No matter where you go—away to college, or maybe somewhere else to live—when you come home, will you visit my husband and me? And if you have kids someday, will you bring them to meet us?"

"Sure I will."

"I want to know about your life, Dennis. I want to see what you do with yourself, and I'd like to grandmother

your children just a little. Is that too strange a thing to ask?"

"No. Not at all." Dennis understood everything now.

"Keep praying for Glen, Dennis, and I will too."

"But . . ."

"I know what you're thinking. I prayed for Gary, and he didn't make it. That's certainly true. But we have to trust. God knows more than we do. He's with us, even when we think He isn't."

"I guess that's right." It was what Dennis had been trying to tell himself.

"I didn't get my son back, but the Lord thought of me this Christmas. He sent you and your mother to me. It may have been a little thing, but He knew it was what I needed, and He made sure you came into my store."

"That's how I felt when I left your store. It was a miracle to me that I could buy that dress. And you're the only one who would have done something like that for me. That's why God sent me to you."

"He was thinking about both of us, Dennis. I know He was. But don't forget me. Just let me love your children a little."

"I will. And I know they'll love you."

Tears were flowing down Mrs. Clifford's cheeks. Dennis had given up altogether on stopping his own tears.

CHAPTER 13

Dennis and his family waited each day for a letter from Glen—or another telegram from the War Department. But two weeks passed and nothing came.

These were quiet days for Dennis. He made the long, cold walk up the hill to school each morning, and two days a week he walked all the way down to the drugstore after school. Mr. Littlefield didn't need him nearly so often this time of year, but that was all right with Dennis. He could have used the money, but work was boring in January with all the busyness of Christmas gone. He also had reading to do for his English class, tests to prepare for, and a research paper to write. But he was having a hard time concentrating on those things. He listened to the news, read the newspaper, kept track of what was happening in the war—and waited. He told himself over and over to accept whatever came, and he tried to believe

he could do that, but more than anything, he wanted to know something for sure.

One thing was becoming clear: Dad was scared too. Dennis saw the concern in his father's face, heard it in his voice. He had started calling home every day after he thought the mail had come, and he had rarely ever done that before. He wasn't drinking, either, or using as much bad language as he always had.

What surprised Dennis most was that two Sundays in a row, without saying anything, Dad had put on his old suit and his new white shirt and walked with the family to church services. Dennis had the feeling that Dad was asking the Lord for help and offering these little changes in his life as proof that he was worth God's attention. Dennis was pretty sure that God didn't think that way, but he understood his dad's intentions; Dennis had been doing the same thing. What touched Dennis most, however, was seeing Dad, just as the church service was beginning, take hold of Mom's hand. Dennis could see that Dad had scrubbed his hands. He hadn't gotten much of the grease out of his skin, but he had obviously tried his best, and Dennis liked to see those rough, dark fingers wrapped around his mother's delicate hand.

Mom wore her new dress each Sunday, but she kept her coat on, and Dennis thought he understood why.

She loved the dress, but he figured she was worried that people would think she was being too fancy, all in lavender blue, looking so pretty.

Everyone at church knew about Glen, and they all asked whether any word about him had come. Dennis wished, in a way, that they wouldn't ask, and yet these people were like family. He had known them all his life, and he heard in their voices that they loved Glen, that they wanted "their boy" to be all right.

Dennis had some good talks with his mother. Mostly, he asked Mom about her feelings, and he listened—the way Mrs. Clifford had told him to do. He noticed, though, that Mom's main concern was for him. She understood how much Glen meant to Dennis, and clearly, she didn't want him to be devastated if and when bad news came.

What Mom did admit was that this new wait was the worst yet. "I just don't understand why they don't let us know something," she told Dennis. "Your dad says it's probably fouled-up paperwork, but I don't know. If he's alive, wouldn't he write to us?"

"I guess. But maybe he was hurt pretty bad and hasn't been able to write."

"Then someone should write a letter for him. Don't they know what we're going through?"

Dennis had no answer. But he didn't tell her not to worry. He knew she couldn't help doing that.

On Wednesday, January 17, Dennis came home from school and tried to finish the reading he had to do for his research paper. He was sitting at the kitchen table when the telephone rang. "Grab that, will you, Dennis?" Mom said.

Dennis tried to finish the paragraph he was reading. He let the phone ring two more times, and then he picked up the receiver. "Hello," he said.

He heard a quiet voice say, "Uh . . . who is this?"

"Dennis."

"Oh, Dennis. You sound so grown up."

And then the world came to a stop. Dennis's breath was suddenly gone. He knew the voice, but he couldn't speak, couldn't think what to do.

"Dennis?"

He let out a gasp, but he still couldn't come up with any words.

"Dennis, is that you?"

"Glen," Dennis finally got out. "Is it you, Glen?"

"Yeah."

Mom was there in an instant. Dennis held the receiver between them and they leaned so close their heads

touched. "Glen, is it you? Are you all right?" Mom was asking.

No answer came for a time, and then, quietly, "Well . . . somewhat."

"Oh, Glen, we've been so worried."

"I sent you a letter—you know, once I got so I could manage it—but then they flew me out. I guess I got to the States before my letter got to you."

"Where are you?"

"Washington, D.C. At Walter Reed—the big military hospital."

"What happened? Are you hurt bad?"

"Well . . . fairly bad. But I'm doing better now."

"Were you shot or what?" Dennis asked.

"It was mortar fire. The shrapnel cut me up pretty bad, and it shattered my knee. I'll have to have surgery once the swelling goes down a little more."

"But you'll be all right, won't you?" Mom asked.

"I hope so." There was a moment's pause. Dennis could sense the change in Glen. He didn't sound like the confident boy who had left Ogden two years back. "Anyway, I'm coming home. They're putting me on a train tomorrow. They'll operate on me out there in Utah. I should be home by Saturday, but I don't have an exact schedule."

"Oh, Glen, I'm so thankful," was all Mom could say. She let her head drop onto her arm, which was bent on the table, and she began to sob.

"Mom?" Glen was saying. Dennis lowered the receiver close to her ear, and he leaned down to it himself.

"Yes?"

"I've been having some trouble. You know, sleeping, and just figuring things out. I don't feel exactly right, I guess you might say."

"That doesn't matter, Glen. You're coming home. I'll help you. Once I have you here, I can make you better."

Glen didn't answer for a long time. Dennis could hear him taking deep breaths. Finally he said, "That's what I need, Mom. I've needed you to take care of me ever since this happened."

"So don't worry. I'll look after you. But how will we know when you're getting here?"

"I'll call you from Denver or somewhere like that."

"Okay. I can't wait to see you. And I can't wait to tell your dad and the girls that you're okay."

"Yeah. It'll be good to see everyone. Just be a little patient with me when I get there. I still need some rest, and . . . I don't know . . . maybe some time to figure out how to be myself again."

"That's okay, Glen. I understand."

"I love you, Mom. You too, Dennis. Good-bye for now. And I'll let you know what time I'm getting in."

"I love you, Glen," Dennis said, but Glen had already hung up. Dennis put the receiver down and looked at his mother.

"He's gone through a lot," she said. "He sounded so different."

"People always say that when they come home they're never the same."

"He doesn't have to be the same. He just has to be okay, and we'll make sure he is."

Dennis felt peace in those words. A powerful sense of relief was settling into his chest. The worst was finally over. "You need to call Dad," he said.

"I know. But first let's have a prayer. We need to thank Heavenly Father."

Dad came home early from work that day. He looked like a different man. He didn't talk a lot, didn't even act like anything had changed, but Dennis saw life in his eyes that hadn't been there for a long time. Linda and Sharon squealed and jumped up and down when they first heard, but in a few minutes they were telling their dolls how much they had missed them all day, and Dennis knew that they didn't really understand what their brother had been through, and they probably never would.

Dennis began a new kind of wait. That night, and again the next day, he tried to study, tried to think about anything else, but the only thing he could think of was his brother getting off that train. On Saturday morning Glen did call from Denver, and that afternoon Dennis rode with his parents and sisters down to the Union Pacific station at the foot of 25th Street. Mom had everyone dress in Sunday clothes. Dennis wore his suit, and Mom wore her new dress—with her coat over it.

As it turned out, a delay somewhere along the line kept the train from getting in until almost eight o'clock. By then the girls were tired and out of sorts from sitting on the hard benches for so many hours, and Dennis was feeling as though he would explode.

Dennis had expected to go out to the loading platform, but with the war on, families were not allowed to do that. So after the train was announced, everyone stood near the entrance to the big waiting hall and watched as passengers began to stream inside, their voices echoing from the vaulted ceiling. Dennis looked at everyone who came in and tried to imagine what Glen might look like now. He had almost decided that his brother wasn't on the train after all when he spotted him straggling behind the others, recognizable because of his limp and his slow pace. He was thin and ghostly pale. A porter was walking

with him, carrying his duffel bag. Mom hurried toward him, and Glen looked at her, but he didn't smile. He held his palms forward to stop her. "Be a little careful," he said.

Mom had surely intended to hug him, but she stood in front of him now, seemingly unsure of what she should do. Glen thanked the porter, a black man in a white smock, who set the bag down and then shook his head when Glen reached in his pocket for a tip. Glen thanked the man again and then turned and took an awkward, off-balance step toward Mom. He wrapped his arms softly around her, as though he were encircling an angel. "Oh, Mom, it's so good to see you," he said. Dad walked forward and picked up the duffel bag, and then he waited. When Glen finally looked at him, Dad extended his hand. Glen was still holding Mom, but he reached over her shoulder and shook hands with him. Dennis had edged closer by then. Glen patted his brother on the shoulder. "Hey, Dennis," he said, and he managed a weak smile. "I think you're taller than I am." Then he let go of Mom and looked at Linda and Sharon, who were keeping their distance. "Girls, you've grown up so much," he said. "Come here."

The girls seemed a little frightened. Glen certainly didn't look like the brother in any of the pictures they had

seen, and it was mostly the pictures they knew now. But they did go to him, and Glen took one of them under each arm and pulled them close to his hips. "I'm finally here," he said. "That train ride took forever. I thought I'd never make it." He was smiling a little better now, but his lips were colorless, and his face was so wasted away that he looked fifty years old.

"Everything will be all right now," Mom said.

Glen nodded, but tears had begun to run down his cheeks. "I don't know how to tell you . . . what's happened to me. I have bad dreams. I can't stand loud noises. I don't sleep very well. I'm worried you're all going to think I've gone crazy."

"It doesn't matter," Dad said. "You're here, and you don't have to go back."

Glen nodded. His eyes didn't seem focused, as though he were thinking back, not seeing what was in front of him. "Lots of times I wondered if I'd ever see any of you again."

"We wondered too," Dad said.

And then Glen did something Dennis hadn't expected. He stepped to Dad, got balanced on his shaky legs, and took Dad into his arms. "A lot of things you taught me helped me stay alive," he told his father. Dennis saw the stiffness come out of Dad. Slowly, he

dropped the duffel bag, and his arms came up around Glen's back. The two stood and embraced that way for a long time.

Dennis watched all this, glad to see it, but he felt distant, not really part of what was happening.

Dad finally stepped back. He ducked his head.

Glen turned to Dennis and hugged him, too. That was almost too much for Dennis. He had waited for this moment for far too long. He cried much harder than he wanted to. He forced himself away before long and tried to get control. But then Dennis moved toward Dad without knowing exactly what would come of that. When Dad saw him so near, he seemed confused. The two looked at each other for a few seconds, and then Dad reached first. Dennis wrapped his arms around his father, and he felt Dad's hands press hard against his back. Dennis held on and sobbed, and when he finally stepped back, he saw tears in his dad's eyes, too.

But neither said anything, and the silence that followed was awkward. No one seemed to know what else to do.

It was Dad who finally said, "Me and Dennis had a talk. When spring comes, the three of us are going to go fishing together."

"That sounds good," Glen said. "Really good. And let's take the girls. Have they ever gone fishing?"

"No, but it's time they learned," Dad said. "And your mom grew up fishing. She can cast as good as I can."

Dennis loved to think of it: all of them together up at the Pineview Reservoir, or maybe on the Ogden River.

"Right now, though, I just want to go home," Glen said. "I'm wearing down."

So Dennis took Glen's duffel bag, and they all walked out to the car, and when they got home, Dennis helped Glen up the steps to the front porch. He was wobbling by the time he got inside, but he made his way to the kitchen. "I've thought so much about being here," he said. "I always pictured us sitting around that big old table, eating dinner. Did you have a turkey for Thanksgiving, and pumpkin pie?"

"We did," Mom said. "And apple for Linda."

Glen laughed. "What about Christmas? Who handed out the presents on Christmas morning?"

"I did," Dennis said. "But you can have your job back next year."

"Sounds good," Glen said, and then he looked around at everyone. "Did you know it was Christmas Day when that mortar shell got me?"

"No, we didn't," Mom said.

"I should've died. But Sid Dibbs, my friend, climbed out of a foxhole in the middle of all that shelling. He tied up my leg and carried me back to an aid station. I didn't know any of that at the time. But he put his life on the line, and he saved mine. I would have bled to death without him."

"We were so worried right then," Mom said. "We knew you were surrounded. We thought about you all that day."

"And prayed," Dennis said.

Glen pulled a chair out from the table and eased himself into it. Dennis could see how exhausted he was. His hands were shaking. "Now Dibbs is still over there," he said. "And I'm sitting at my kitchen table. So many of my friends . . ." But he didn't finish the sentence. He just stared at his hands, now gripped together on top of the table.

Mom said, "You offered your life, honey, the same as every soldier—that's all that really matters. We just have to be grateful that God brought you back to us."

Sharon had edged closer to Glen. She leaned her head so she could see his face, and she said, "I prayed you'd come home for Christmas, and you almost did."

He smiled and touched her hair. "I hardly know you, little sister," Glen said. "You're such a big girl now."

Clearly Linda wanted to be part of that. She pressed close to Glen on his other side.

"Both of you are," he said. "You're such pretty girls."

"Mom's the pretty one," Linda said. "Did you see what she got for Christmas?"

Mom still had her coat on, but she unbuttoned it now and slipped it off.

Glen turned in his chair to look at her. "Mom, you're beautiful," he said. "What a perfect dress!"

"Show him how it shines. Spin around," Dennis said.

Mom turned all the way around.

Glen used the table to brace himself, and he stood up. "At the train station, I noticed something," he said. "And I just caught a whiff again when you turned like that. You still wear that lavender stuff you used to wear."

Mom smiled. "Of course I do," she said. "It's what I've always worn."

"When I was in Holland, I saw a huge field of plants with purple blossoms. I broke off a little stem from one of them and smelled it, and then I knew what it was—because it smelled like you. It was lavender. I kept some in my pocket for a long time because it made me think of you. But look at you now. You're dressed in the same color as that field I saw."

"I call it lavender blue," Dennis said.

"Spin around faster," Linda urged. "The way you did on Christmas."

Mom spun around once, twice, three times. The lavender-blue dress gleamed, and by the time she had stopped turning, Mom's face was shining, too.

Dennis was so glad that he and Dad had given Mom a dress that pleased her so much. But now she had her real Christmas gift, sent from God. When she finished spinning, she took Glen in her arms one more time.

By then, Dennis was praying again. He thanked God for hearing him, for knowing him, for caring about Glen—and for his family.